The Great Work
A Scenic Journey Through Life

Thomas Lyons

Editor: Beverly Pearl

Photo preparation (internal): Alina Hromko
https://www.hromkoalina.photography/
https://www.instagram.com/hromkoalina.photography/

Cover Design: Alina Hromko

ISBN: 978-1-927974-45-2

© *2025, Thomas Lyons*
All rights reserved.

Acknowledgements

I dedicate this work to the memory of my late wife, Eileen, partner, confidant, mentor and friend who regrettably passed on in 2023. In her honour, I have included several pieces of her writing, a joint effort on the Canal du Midi, Fr. and her comments on Trinidad's Carnival or Mas.

We shared so much together over a period of almost 60 years as we journeyed and opened and closed doors together making most of the following stories possible.

Eileen was entirely non-judgmental, and had the innate ability to make others feel at ease and to be able to express themselves. She cared about and valued each and every friend along the way—a valuable asset on a shared journey.

I would also acknowledge our family, Kelly and Ken, Patrick, Grands, Liam and Meghan and their respectives, Dominique and Adam. Kelly read my first draft for me, and Patrick was my back-up techie, which with my computer mind was much-needed.

I would be remiss in not mentioning our family and connections in Ireland, England, Trinidad, Costa Rica and Ontario, all of whom have, in our interactions, had an impact on the journey.

It would also be appropriate to acknowledge, in this increasingly interactive world, the many people we encountered along the way in a wide variety of capacities: the Indigenous ladies in Ontario and Surinam, the workshop participants in China, Denmark, Egypt, Kenya, Ontario and Eastern Europe, plus my new Ukrainian family of Alina and her two children, all of whom had an impact on our lives and the ultimate journey.

Lastly, but definitely not least, I would like to acknowledge my great-granddaughter, Sage, who at seven

Acknowledgements

months cannot yet handle the text, but in later life will be able to read the text and have an understanding about her great-grandparents.

Dedicated to my loving wife, Eileen

Foreword

Thomas Lyons

During my reflections at Eileen's Celebration of Life I expressed to the assembled gathering about how fortunate we had been in finding each other, and about how brilliant our journey together had been. Lovely family, great friends and adventures. I also commented that I thought we had travelled

Foreword

along the scenic route in life with a few bumps along the way. Along this journey we encountered many wonderful people and a myriad of situations, which I would comment on as stories at festive occasions, perhaps lubricated with a beverage of choice. People would say "Tom, you should write them down," and I would nod my head in concurrence, but never did, until now. I don't know if it was the passing of Eileen, or the birth of my first great-grandchild, Sage, that motivated me, but here we are ... a book about various situations that I encountered and my comments. We have also provided a website book of coloured photographs covering some of the journey, bearing in mind that the possession of a good camera does not a photographer make.

~~ *Thomas Lyons*

About the Author

Thomas Lyons is a former Teacher, Department Head, Provincial Coordinator and independent Consultant with Educational Awareness.

A graduate in Economic and Human geography from The Queen's University of Belfast, he came to Canada on a post graduate fellowship and then entered the teaching profession. He found that he liked working with young people, both as a teacher and a coach.

A two-year stint with the Canadian International Development Agency in Trinidad and Tobago had a profound effect, and changed his outlook on life, and his views on how our human world had evolved. It gave him a new purpose in Life.

Thomas completed a Masters degree specializing in the educational needs of Developing Nations, and became involved with a number of Non-government Organizations. Eventually this led to his position as the Coordinator of Education For a Global Perspective in Ontario through OTF and CIDA.

Upon retirement, Thomas worked closely with his partner, Eileen, on a number of projects, both in Canada and abroad, and spent time in Armenia, China, Egypt, Georgian Republic, Kenya, Serbia, Tanzania, and Ukraine.

They delivered workshops at conferences in Ontario, California, Denmark, and Costa Rica, and with Indigenous Women in Ontario.

They were partners in a small fruit farm in Costa Rica, in which the fruits of their labour were provided to local seniors residences.

Thomas and Eileen also lived in France, and travelled widely on vacations to Ireland, Europe, UK and the Caribbean.

Prologue

As I approach the latter days of my passage on this phenomenal planet, I am truly amazed at the very existence of life as we know it. I don't know whether to laugh or cry as I behold the many wonders that surround me and the many disasters caused by the actions of my species. At times, I wonder what our purpose is within the universe.

A former mentor of mine, namely Thomas Berry, a Passionist priest, Asian scholar, Geologian, and student of the Universe Story, commented that the role of the human was to tell the story of the universe. This is why I despair as I ponder which story to tell.

As a result of my pondering, I have settled on the only one that makes any kind of sense, and that is my story as I best recall it.

OK? Here we go on a scenic journey through life.

The weight of the world.
Design by Tom Goldsmith Art
tomgoldsmithart, at Instagram

On The Web

I was recently shocked to find out that I have over 20,000 photographs on my computer, and I am still missing my wonderful pictures of Mas in Trinidad. Given our Planet Earth is a veritable rainbow of colours, I felt that the book required some colour, but colour is prohibitively expensive. Enter the Tech-World, and the mind of my Ukrainian friend Alina, who said, "Why don't you create a website that readers can access through a QR code?"

With the help of Stephan Sokolow, here it is:

Companion to "The Great Work: A Scenic Journey Through Life"

https://archive.org/details/the-great-work-companion

By using your phone on the QR code you can enter a world that has, to some extent, paralleled the chapters of the book, with some additions. Not all the photographs have captions, e.g., some buildings, beach scenes, some people—but the country of origin is included.

Table of Contents

Acknowledgements	i
Foreword	iii
About the Author	v
Prologue	vi
On The Web	vii
Beginnings	1
The Two Solitudes	5
Childhood Years	11
Formal Education	17
Across the Big Pond	21
Land of the Brave	29
Adventures in Public Education	33
Career Advancement	43
The Caribbean	49
Excursion to Venezuela	67
Excursion to Suriname	73
Trinidad Shenanigans	83
Back to Normality	93
Our Year in Languedoc	97
Education From a Global Perspective (EGP)	107
Costa Rica	119
Egypt	125
The Asian Component of our Journey	135
Musings from a Boat on the Canal du Midi, 2006	143
Myth and Reality	149
Family Jaunts	159
Les Belles Isles	161
Appendix	163
Afterword	164

Chapter I

Beginnings

As I relate some tales that affected my passage along the scenic route of life with a few wrinkles or bumps, I am reminded that my journey might have been cut short but for the foresight of my astute father.

My parents were married in 1938, and at that time his mother owned a bakery and two shops located in working class areas of Belfast, namely the Newtonards Road and Donegal Pass. In those times, the standard procedure was for men to bring their weekly wages home and hand them over to the wife. She removed the necessary funds for household expenses such as food, rent and insurance, then handed him his beer and smokes money plus incidentals. The result was that there was always food on the table, and my grandmother's shops were very busy, as she baked first class "stuff". I do remember acting as a doorman for line-ups on a Saturday at the Donegal Pass shop.

When my parents married, his mother offered them the apartment/flat located above the bakery/shop on the Newtonards Road. My forward-thinking father astutely realized that there was a payback for this act of generosity, if anything went wrong with the baking equipment, shop fittings, etc, he would be called upon to make the necessary repairs, no questions asked. He was a first class plumber by trade and very "handy", but valued his independence and respectfully declined the offer.

If truth be told, I remember accompanying him on many emergencies to the shop/bakery in Donegal Pass, where my role as a child was to help clean up. Why not at the premises on the Newtonards Road, you ask? Well that is the point of my digression. On the night of the 1941

Beginnings

German bombing of Belfast, those premises took a direct hit and were obliterated and so, if not for my father's desire for independence, my life would have been quite short.

My grandmother did not own the land (she paid ground rent to the Church) and she did not rebuild on that site, which remained vacant for years. My grandmother had been a shade unlucky. The German intended targets were Harland and Wolf's, the world's largest shipyard, and the neighbouring aircraft factory, which I believed had limited damage, while thousands of houses, Granny's bakery and flat, and scores of church spires were demolished. About 1000 people perished in the attack.

The anti- aircraft batteries ceased firing at the Junkers in case they hit RAF planes. Problem was, the RAF weren't there, and so the Germans had a few hours of unfettered bombing and lots of churches to destroy.

As an aside, many years later I flew from Canada for my father's funeral, and as we waited outside the church for the procession to form, an elderly gentleman came up to me and introduced himself.

He said, "You don't know me, but I know you, for your father always talked about you. I just wanted to tell you that today we are burying the last HONEST PLUMBER in Ireland."

I only wish he had passed on his skill set to me as I can barely afford a plumber nowadays. It's amazing how little you get for $1000.00 today.

Years earlier, shortly after my partner and I had moved into our first house, the toilets were blocked, and I, trained only in cleaning up after the job was completed, was at a loss as to how to proceed. Was the problem within the house or outside on municipal property?

I solved my dilemma by calling both a Yellow Pages plumber and the municipality. The plumber arrived first

Beginnings

and started "snaking" the toilets, and then the municipality showed up. Their foreman, in a thick Ulster accent, told me that he thought it was my problem, but upon further chatting he discovered that his instructor at the Belfast College of Technology was my Dad. He couldn't do enough for me. He told me to pay off the plumber, whom he considered to be useless, and they found the problem for me at no charge. A child had flushed a teddy bear down a basement toilet. It was not their problem, but because of the good work of my Dad it was fixed and no charge, and I now knew where my drains were.

Air raid damage in Belfast
Collection at the Imperial War Museum, London

Chapter II
The Two Solitudes

Growing up in Northern Ireland was to embrace a tribal culture. You had the two major divides namely the Catholic and Protestant separation. However, the Protestants were further divided into Church of Ireland, Presbyterians, Methodists, Baptists, Seventh Day Adventists and assorted evangelical groups.

Everyone went to church on Sundays as part of the tribal ritual. That's an interesting comparison to today where many of the churches are quite empty on a Sunday, as religion has a hard time competing with Ryanair and weekends in Barcelona.

Each church group had its own youth organizations, church committees, women's groups and each operated within its perceived rules and deeply felt distrust of competing Christian groups. The main two divides lived in splendid isolation with separate churches, separate hospitals, separate dance halls, separate neighbourhoods, separate cemeteries, and separate histories, each with a different story to tell.

To me a classic example occurs every July 12th ... the Glorious Twelfth or Orange-men's Day, when hundreds of men wearing orange sashes, or collarettes, parade in N.I. Accompanied by silver, pipe, brass, and flute bands they march to show unity and solidarity with fellow protestants, but also to intimidate the Catholic population.

The organization officially formed in 1795 after years of internecine vigilantism. Its main purpose was to unite the Protestant community against Catholicism, and to ensure the position of N.I. under the British crown, and today within the United Kingdom.

It took its name and standard-bearer from Protestant William of Orange and his historic victory over the

The Two Solitudes

Catholic James 11 of England at the Battle of the Boyne, Ireland in 1690. Ironically despite its strong chants of "No Pope here" the Pope played a major financial role in fundraising for William's army.

The marchers and Lodge members have never been taught the actual background to the struggle. Catholicism was not the issue. The real enemy was Louis X1V and his military dominance in Europe. Amongst other things he wanted his own Pope on the Papal Throne, and his armies threatened William' homeland of the Netherlands. James was supported by Louis. Furthermore, the dominant elites of England did not want James on the English throne.

The army itself was a mixed bag, with at least one third consisting of German Catholic mercenaries from Saxony, and some of the Dutch soldiers were probably Catholic as well. So the annual marchers, with some 18 parades on the 12th, are living a massive contradiction, and it's not that they don't care; they are simply ignorant as no one has ever told them. It was not taught in schools to either group.

Cemeteries, you say. Well I was once told by a nice unionist lady of a certain age, that things in "Norn Iron" were going to the "dogs". When asked to explain, she replied that there were Catholics in Protestant cemeteries now.

Upon further analysis, I figured out what she was referring to. In North Belfast on the foothills of the Antrim plateau there were two cemeteries: a Catholic one on the upside of the slope, and a Protestant beneath it.

Now, the soils of the area were created from glacial clay deposited some 10,000 years ago and clay, occasionally, has been known to slide along sheer planes within the ground. This can be facilitated, if there is surplus water present within the soil profile. Not that there is ever a surplus of rain water in Ulster! As a result, the coffins, with their remains, had moved with the clay down the slope underground, and slid under the wall and into the Protestant burial ground. This was certainly not in the heavenly direction originally intended and did cause a certain consternation within the respective communities.

We tried to assure the dear lady that she had nothing to concern herself about as there were no Catholics or Protestants in cemeteries, only remains.

The protestant tribes did mix with one another, but although it happened, it was difficult to cross the major divide because of the strong emotional antithesis between Catholics and Protestants. I was at one time somewhat dazzled by a gorgeous, young Catholic girl, and we went out briefly. However, I could never go within a mile or two of her home and when she sent me a Christmas card, which apparently my sister opened by mistake, my mother and she both quizzed me to know who Kathleen was?

Kathleen tended to be a name associated with Catholic girls, although the protestant lady next door was also Kathleen. Perhaps this could be explained by the fact that she came from Dublin.

There is one moment in time that I know of where both Catholics and Protestants joined forces, and it was a very brief moment in time. I learned about it not in Belfast, but through watching a TV program on the Ontario, Canada, Educational Network.

The early thirties were terrible times for the unemployed in the western world. The Wall Street collapse and subsequent Great Depression had led to terrible living conditions and starvation in working class neighbourhoods in Belfast, and finally people had enough. The Outdoor Relief Riots in October 1932 began in Catholic neighbourhoods in West Belfast. Rioters attacked the institutions of Government, buses, etc. The police, guns drawn, were overwhelmed. When news reached the

The Two Solitudes

Protestant working class streets, who, suffering the same conditions, then joined in, and they fought the police together.

A moment of unity and class interest had miraculously overcome traditional animosity. Ulster army regiments were mobilized, but could they be trusted? And so, soldiers were imported from Scotland, a typical Imperial ploy. After three days, the riots were quelled.

The aftermath was really fascinating and clearly illustrates the Ulster issues. At Mass, the following Sunday, the priests stood up and warned their flock that they were toying with "Godless Communism."

The Catholic Church hierarchy in Armagh spoke out strongly in condemnation of the events. In the Protestant Churches the Ministers strongly spoke out against the events and issued a dire warning,

"You people don't know what you are doing. Those people want you jobs."

The status quo was saved. The power brokers were still in control and class consciousness almost disappeared and has never been much of a political force in N.I. Politics. None of this is ever taught in schools.

It reminds me a bit of the USA, where people who hardly have a "pot to pee" in vote for multimillionaires, in the mistaken belief that the super rich have their best interest at heart. It could be argued that religion plays a similar role as in N.I, by encouraging the populace to focus on a heavenly God, enriching Pastors and the life hereafter and not on existing conditions. Note how after every mass shooting in the USA, the political elite are first in line praying for the victims. They never take on the wealth and power of the gun lobby to address the issue of ease and availability of guns in their society.

I have often wondered, even if he/she is omnipotent, how the devil does he/she have the time to sort out who

The Two Solitudes

will win the myriad sporting fixtures each weekend in the USA, never mind dealing with the rest of the Universe.

In N.I. the role of the tribal church was paramount. In fact the worst thing you could be was to have no religion at all. A university acquaintance of mine had an interview with Belfast Council's Education Committee for a position in one of their schools. When asked as to why he had not completed the space on the application form for religion, he replied that he was an atheist. He was quickly ushered out the door.

In my own case, as an Honours Geography student about to graduate, I applied for a teaching position at a leading Ulster Grammar School. I should point out that I was the only student from my graduating year to apply. Catholic classmates could not apply to a Protestant school and most of the others were on a combined scholarship, which meant that upon graduation, they had to complete a one-year Education Diploma course. However, one did not need this to teach, and so I applied. In addition, I had been a fairly successful school athlete in rugby and track having been a member of teams that had won the only two annual Cup/Shield competitions in school's rugby and had success in the short sprints. I had also written my undergraduate Honours thesis on a comparative development of the pig/bacon industries of Northern Ireland and Denmark, and had spent some time in Denmark.

During my interview, the Headmaster noticed the Danish reference and told me that the school trip later that year was going to be in Denmark. Since the teacher leading the excursion had no previous experience in that country, he wondered if I would be willing to talk with her. I, of course, was delighted to oblige, and he left to relieve her to meet with me.

The Two Solitudes

I spent about 40 mins talking with her about what to expect, and some dos and don'ts, and she left beaming. The Headmaster returned also beaming, and I subsequently left the interview beaming. I was set for life working at a good school, great neighbourhood, good pay ... what more could I want?
I DID NOT GET THE JOB.

I forgot to mention that for these jobs one needed a letter from one's Church minister. I had one of those, and it was a great recommendation, but it was signed by my lowly RECTOR. Several weeks after I received the disappointing news I had a call from him in which he apologized for letting me down. I asked him to explain, and he told me that he had been outranked by a BISHOP. Apparently a Bishop's nephew had got the job with only a pass degree (no Honours), no sports background, no Denmark.

Shortly after that I decided that life in N.I. was not for me and accepted a scholarship to a Canadian university. Another step along the scenic journey.

Chapter III
Childhood Years

At the time, I believed that I had had a great childhood. Situated on an island some distance from Britain, German bombings were rare. With our own chickens and my father's connections within the Irish Republic, we had few food issues during the war. There were lots of children living in the neighbourhood, and weather wise we could spend a lot of time outside where we created our own activities without adult interference. Mothers weren't worried as there was not much traffic and deliveries were mainly by horse, and cart and later electric vans.

In 2023, I visited Northern Ireland for a family funeral, and dropped in to see an older cousin who had not been able to attend the funeral. It was a great visit as we went down memory lane to the years during and just after the second World War. The conversation both opened the eyes and ears of my daughter and nephew, who were also there, as we seemed to remember different events at different times.

When we left, my cousin said to me, "Tom, we didn't have much, did we?"

I concurred, and then she said "But we sure had fun didn't we?"

I smiled and agreed.

I have often wondered where the electric vans went, as they had to be reinvented at great expense many years later. They had, of course, been eased out by diesel trucks, and I have always wondered if that was a major cause of the increase in cancers in family life.

Tuberculosis (TB) was the major health issue in my day. There were specialized TB hospitals. I was for a while home bound as a suspected patient, and was inoculated against the disease. Some years later, when

Childhood Years

Great childhood in Northern Ireland. Every summer the family spent two weeks at the beach in Newcastle.

Childhood Years

visiting N.I., I observed that TB was no longer a problem after the milk cows were vaccinated, but the specialized hospital had not closed. It was now full of cancer patients and every other hospital had a cancer ward. Why had cancer spread so quickly? What were we adding to the air?

Mind you, shopping habits have also changed. My mother used to go "down the road" several days a week. She often walked and took the bus when it rained. On her quest, she chatted with friends and visited stores, where the shopkeepers knew her by name.

Try introducing yourself to a supermarket clerk today and see how far that gets you.

The butcher cut her favourite cuts of meat, from beef hung in his cold store. The green grocer sold her the vegetables and fruit that were in season, plus others from a small range of imports. She might visit the newsagents and the sweet shop. Milk and bread were delivered to the door, initially by horse and cart, then by electric vehicles, and later still in diesel vans.

It should be noted that most goods were fresh, containing no additives to add artificial flavours or expand the life of the product. Furthermore, no plastic was used—only paper, and my Mum carried her own shopping bags. I must add that by that visit.

My mother rarely went down the road, and my father was driving her once a week to purchase goods in the supermarket. They now had a refrigerator to store the chemical foodstuffs wrapped in plastic. I wonder if we ever really know what we are doing. That is not to say that in certain environments fridges are essential.

The key ingredient in my growing up was the fact that we made our own fun with what little we had. No social media, no games modules, no TV, no cell phones, no Toys or US. In fact, I am certain that there were no home phones —just a pay phone box on the major street. But we had fun,

Childhood Years

especially when they removed the air raid shelters from the street. Then we could play street games such as football/soccer (sometimes with a soup can when the ball burst), tag, hide-and-seek, and games of rounders, and bicycle races. I am not sure that the older teenage kids wanted the shelters removed, as the dark, windowless shelters were ideal for the shenanigans that teenagers experimented with.

Ah, such is the joy of life as one only truly learns through experimentation. The Yanks think that they invented baseball, but they really only copied rounders and added the multi-million dollar salaries, beer, and hot dogs.

It is interesting that after I had been in Canada for a while, my parents came for a visit. My father had been a keen sports watcher ,and had been a harrier and cyclist in his day, so I took him to a Canadian football game. He was quickly bored out of his skull. He could not grasp the need for separate offensive and defensive squads, hated the constant stop start of the game, and we left at 90 minutes—the length of time of an average soccer game.

Some years later, when major league baseball came to Toronto, I took him to a Blue Jays game, and he loved it. It was ROUNDERS, so he understood it. If I remember right, he also had a beer and a hot dog, and stayed through all nine innings.

Childhood Years

My sister Betty and I on the slides, in Newcastle, Co. Down.

Chapter IV
Formal Educational

In our societies, universal primary education has been the norm since the 19th century, and as a result, with most people having some experience at a school, everyone's an expert on schools and learning. When I commenced at age five, schools were very different from today. Discipline was strict; corporal punishment was common; writing out of hundreds of lines (sentences such as "I must not be late for class", were common), and teachers were always right. At least that's what my father said.

Having spent a good portion of my working life in education I could comment on that, but perhaps not. I commented one time to my fellow inmate at secondary school that, given my current experience, if I was a school administrator I would not have hired many of my former teachers. He became upset, and I thought that my former school chum was going to ask me to leave his car and walk.

I don't remember much about primary school except that it was a good school, in a "good" neighbourhood, with the major emphasis placed on getting as many students as possible to pass the Qualifying Exams. They determined the type of schooling one would receive in your teenage years, and the school's reputation. A Pass enabled one to go to a Grammar School, where the emphasis was placed on maths, sciences, languages, Latin, history and geography, and "posh" sports such as rugby for the boys and field hockey or lacrosse for girls.

A "Fail" sent one off to an Intermediate School until age 16, where the emphasis was on skills training in the Trades and Office needs, such as shorthand typing.

Formal Education

The inherent problems and contradictions were never addressed, and I well remember the family pressure and the home atmosphere both at exam time, and especially at results time. Often students had to repeat the year. An acquaintance of mine failed the X1 plus exam, but his father had the finances to send him to grammar school as a private, fee-paying student. He successfully passed A Levels and entered University, and the last I heard he was a university professor somewhere.

Schooling was a selection system with many frailties, and the pass rate for the X1 Plus exam depended on the number of places available at the Grammar School level. Another flaw was that these exam systems treat every human the same instead of as a unique individual.

The inherent class system came to the fore in sports. Games such as Soccer, the game for the working classes, was the major boy's sport of the Intermediate Schools, and I guess the girls also played hockey. Catholic schools played Gaelic games and possibly soccer, but never having been inside one, I can't be accurate. I learnt to play rugger, which I initially hated, as the games-teacher placed me in the sweaty, smelly, rough scrum, and at age 11 I was somewhat of a delicate flower. It was only at 13 when I was bigger, and developed into a sprinter. I enjoyed the game as a "flying winger", playing on school teams.

Some things stand out from that time. As I was relatively small at age 11, and also had ginger hair, I was bullied and was unhappy at school. My marks reflected unhappiness. At 13, still with ginger hair, I was the flying winger. The bullying stopped, and my marks went up. I even had a nickname .... "Leo", which followed me throughout the rest of my school days, and I was addressed as such by both boys and staff.

Formal Education

Another path on the scenic route of life I should mention is that there were other school sports programs, especially indoor sports. I merely mention the main ones. Indeed, I was very surprised to find out in 2023 that a contemporary of mine, Allan Moneypenny had played professional basketball in Europe and the NBA.

Experiential learning rarely occurred, and even science labs were tightly controlled. Can you imagine the girls of St Trinians' unsupervised in a lab? "Safety First", would hardly be the order of the day.

Schooling was well described by Marshall McLuhan when he talked about driving into the future while looking in the rearview mirror. Schooling was essentially the learning of what society already knew and as a result there could be nothing new. From my perspective it was actually worse, as I, with a 54% Irish DNA, was actually being altered into something foreign.

The imported grammar school model was designed to create little middle class English boys and girls. Indigenous peoples can relate to this in considering the function of Residential Schools. They at least knew what was being done to them, causing great unhappiness, but with us it was more insidious. We went willingly and loudly.

Imagine the following occurrence in daily school assemblies: a 700 Northern Irish male voice choir singing lustily, "Rule Britannia, Britannia rules the waves, England never, never, never, shall be slaves," or

> "And did those feet in ancient time
> walk upon England;s mountains green?
> And was the holy lamb of God
> On England's pleasant pastures seem?
> And did the Countenance Divine
> Shine forth upon our clouded hills?

Formal Education

> And was Jerusalem builded here
> Amongst those dark Satanic mills?"

This hymn, based on an epic poem by William Blake, was published in 1808. The orchestration, arranged by Sir Edward Edgar, was very powerful stuff, and undoubtedly had a definitive acculturating influence on the delicate and not-so-delicate minds of 11 to 18-year-old Northern Irish youth. We must also not forget that great, British patriotic song, "Land of Hope and Glory", also arranged by Elgar, and published in 1901:

> "Land of Hope and Glory, Mother of the Free,
> How shall we extol thee, who are born of thee?
> Wider still and wider shall thy bounds be set;
> God, who made thee mighty, make thee mightier yet,
> God, who made thee mighty, make thee mightier yet."

Then to crown it all off, no pun intended, there was the Royal Anthem, "God save the King/Queen". This was very powerful stuff, and I have to say that by the time I had completed grammar school. I was aiming for a career in the British Imperial Civil Service.

I don't remember if this influenced me to study Geography at Queen's University, Belfast, but I do remember feeling that, not only did Africa need me, Africa could not exist without me. Lucky for Africa, by the time I graduated from Queen's, most colonial territories had become independent nations and former Governors had become university Dons, unemployed or retired to their English estates, accompanied by their elephant feet umbrella stands. Yuk ...

This also meant that I had to spend my largess elsewhere and be catapulted by other forces along this scenic journey, but at least thanks to my grammar school upbringing, I never had to work in those dark satanic mills.

Chapter V
Across the Big Pond

It was a dark and drizzly night when the Belfast-Glasgow ferry slipped away from the Belfast pier on its daily overnight sail to Scotland. My parents and girlfriend stood somewhat lonely on the quay, as the waters of Belfast Lough lapped against the concrete and wooden structure.

Not many passengers were aboard on a Thursday evening, and I stretched out in the lounge with those not willing or able to pay the extra for a tiny cabin. I settled in with a cup of strong tea to warm me up whilst many of my male companions settled down with bottles of Stout, a thick black liquid that somewhat resembled tar.

It was a smooth crossing compared to some I had made. At times it is so rough, causing a lot of sea sickness, so much so that crew members have to hose down the decks. Once while sheltering on deck during a storm, a woman beside me slipped on the deck, grabbed my leg, and yelled "mister, mister, save me, save me!"

She survived, and after that I chose to fly, except on this trip as I had some luggage.

Off to Canada ...

I had arrived back in Belfast a few weeks before to get my stuff in order, as I had been offered, and accepted, a full scholarship at McMaster University in Hamilton, Ontario. Although it had started off as a Theology College it was now a regular university, and even had a nuclear reactor in the Physics Building. Unlike my job hunting experiences in Ulster, I could not be outranked by a Bishop.

While walking along Donegall Place, a week before my departure, I noticed an office sign on a building, which said "CONSULATE OF CANADA". Wow, maybe I

Across the Big Pond

should go up and see if they have anything I need. As a scholarship recipient I would be offered a one-year Student Visa at my port of entry, namely Montreal, but maybe they had some maps, a geographer's tool.

The young man in the office welcomed me and asked me if I required any help. I explained my situation, and then he 'put a spanner in the works', or alternatively, 'threw me a curved ball.' He asked me an important question: "Why don't you go as a landed immigrant?"

Having been momentarily taken aback and made a hurried sign of the Cross, I asked the big question ... why? It had never crossed my mind.

"It's quite simple," he said. " If you go to Canada, like it and want to stay, as a student you would have to leave and apply from outside the country. As a landed immigrant, you could simply stay—no questions asked. Also, it would not affect your current nationality."

I had to think for a moment or two. Remember, I was still under the influence of the powerful brainwashing effect of "Rule Britannia" and "Land of Hope and Glory", and the idea of becoming a different citizen was almost overwhelming.

However, as I sit at my desk in Orillia, Ontario, some 62 years later, it is obvious that I made the right choice. My parents had great holidays out here, although my existing personal relationship did not survive.

I asked him what was required. Simply your existing passport and a medical exam, which you can have at 2:00 pm today. So a few thumps on the knees, a stethoscope to the chest, and 20 mins later, I had "landed Immigrant" stamped in my passport. NO MONEY changed hands. Considering what one has to do today to achieve that status, and the financial obligation involved, I was continuing along my "scenic journey".

Across the Big Pond

Due to the glassy smooth sailing from Belfast, we landed at Glasgow around 5:30 in the morning. There, at the gangplank waiting for me, was my father's colleague and friend, Davy. After a harbour café greasy breakfast, we headed to the International Pier area to embark on the SS Ramore Head, bound for Chicago, with a short stop in Montreal to drop off eight passengers. She would be floating high on this trip, as the cargo comprised E-Type Jaguars, Singer Sewing Machines, and Scotch Whiskey. The inclusion of sewing machines was somewhat ironic as they were invented in Chicago.

Departure turned out not to be imminent. Apparently a skid had mysteriously malfunctioned, allowing crates of Scotch to become dislodged, causing some breakages. As the cleanup process had apparently involved the consumption of the said beverage, the ship's departure was delayed by three days.

Such is life on the fast track, which resulted in me accompanying Davy, a technical demonstrator in heating and welding technology, on his rounds to Glasgow's dark, satanic mills. As a point of interest, this industrial/port landscape is all gone now. The pier I sailed from sits empty, rain swept and forlorn. The mills were long abandoned, or rebuilt as blocks of flats or shopping centres. The air is now breathable, and the city centre sits resplendent with colourful, polished, Red Sandstone stones.

At sea at last, all eight passengers were sequestered in a basic, but comfortable, lounge, as we reviewed the 'disaster procedures', sipping the Officers' supply of that Scottish beverage. Cabins were spacious, and our meals would be served with the officers.

Intimacy was the order of the day. You could wander anywhere on the ship, the Bridge, Engine Room, and

Across the Big Pond

Radio Room. That was about it—no swimming pool, just a jet black ocean—no TV room—no pool table—no bar with entertainment, but there was a steward always willing to serve up a beverage of choice. One did get to know one's fellow passengers if they were willing, and on some trips that certainly happened. On the previous trip there had been six single New Zealand girls, and according to one of the officers, no one slept alone after the first night at sea. The trip took six days in total, so to paraphrase a pirate captain, there was much "friggin in the riggin."

On the "cruise", I was introduced to two new global phenomena, namely icebergs and the Cold War. I spent a lot of time on board ship in the radio room. The operator was a nice guy, and he liked to talk. I was curious about the communication system and the inter ship communications, and I also helped him record messages and check the football results.

As we approached the external limit of Canadian National waters, the electronic equipment in the room started making loud crackling sounds, and we could hear no messages. Apparently we were approaching a Soviet "fishing fleet" anchored in International waters. It consisted of a large factory ship and a number of trawlers, ostensibly fishing, but in reality listening to radio communications within North America.

Could they also tap into the underwater cables? Lest that upsets you, it is perhaps "comforting" to know that Ottawa was also listening to international calls made by Canadian citizens. Unfortunately I did not know the buzz words to send the system berserk, every time I phoned my parents. My response to the door knocking RCMP would have been "the devil made me do it."

The icebergs at the mouth of the Strait of Belle Isle, close to Newfoundland, were a much quieter affair, but no less impressive. Coming from the home of the Titanic, one's first berg is suitably impressive. These blue/grey late summer bergs venture south along the Labrador/Greenland Sea corridor driven by ocean currents, every year, and may be destined for extinction in the near future with global warming and the demise of the ice-caps.

The sail from Belle Isle to Montreal was uneventful—no whales unfortunately, but it did reinforce the knowledge that parts of Canada are heavily forested, although not with an original forest cover, and that the country is huge. The original forest cover must have been truly amazing to the likes of Champlain and others.

It took over two days to arrive at our destination, and four days to cross the Atlantic. After the prerequisite customs and immigration checks, three of us headed to the Central Station and a cursory look at Montreal. Little did I know that on my second Xmas in Canada, I would fall madly in love with a delightful 19-year-old woman from Montreal, and be engaged on our fourth date. I didn't believe in wasting time while travelling the scenic route through life.

On the CN train to Toronto, I was introduced to the efficiency and commitment of the Canadian state to passenger train travel ... NOT. We left Montreal about 20 minutes late, but after many stops in the middle of nowhere, apparently so as not to slow freight trains, we arrived in Toronto almost two-hours late, and I missed the last train to Hamilton.

Luckily for me, a fellow ship's passenger from Belfast was being met by her daughter and son, and their respective spouses. Her daughter and husband not only took me to Hamilton, but kept me as their guest for a week until I was settled in a student residence. Their generosity helped set a pattern for us. Over the years we have provided shelter for other people, including a young German couple, a Chilean refugee family after the military coup, and now a Ukrainian family escaping the horrors of Putin. Another step on the scenic route of life.

The husband, Frank, to help me settle, introduced me to a distinctive Canadian cultural trait, namely the "Men Only" section of a Tavern. This took me a while to get used to after the more civilized, cultured atmosphere of the UK pub.

The comfortable Irish pub at Sneem with Eileen and my friends Rod and Sue contrasts starkly with the men's taverns of Ontario in 1962.

These spaces seemed to me to be more of a disgusting relic of a form of drinking, which said, "We want your money, so drink, but heaven forbid that you feel comfortable while doing it." Was it the sawdust on the floor or the sheer size and the amount of smoke? Was it the flotilla of servers constantly on the move with their

Across the Big Pond

aluminum trays, overloaded with eight-ounce glasses of a light, amber liquid that passed for beer? The latter was dispatched with great haste to each customer, each receiving at least four glasses each time.

The sole purpose of these establishments was to get one to guzzle as much beer as possible—environs be damned. It seemed to me that there was some kind of inherent punishment involved while you drink until you're soused—the very antithesis of a British pub. The ladies, of course, were to be spared this image of men by being segregated in a 'Ladies and Escort' room. Needless to say, on my first few visits to local taverns, I was quickly inebriated. A slight bump on the scenic journey ...

Chapter VI
Land of the Brave

If you had seen the look of sheer terror in my eyes the first time I donned ice skates ... or any time for that matter ... or glimpsed the former "flying winger" tumbling down the beginner slopes at the Blue Mountain Ski Resort, you would have realized that bravery was out of the question. Eventually I did become somewhat proficient at cross-country skiing as a family activity, and learnt how to throw up guards as a lead in a small curling league, but winter was not really my thing.

One interesting fact is that in my first few years I really didn't feel the cold, and I wonder if it was because I grew up in a comfortable home, but one without central heating. On cold nights one went to bed with a hot water bottle, and in the morning one's mum had placed the coats in front of the fire. After a few years of central heating I was no longer inured to cold temperatures, and religiously wrapped myself up like the rest of the denizens of the brave new world.

I eventually left the university because of a personality clash with the narrow-minded head of department, whom I considered to be inefficient. He alternatively did not warm to me as I had been appointed to the university in his absence. He had been off doing missionary work in Haiti and had not been consulted, and we all know how successful the missionary work has been. In addition, he made a serious mistake with regard to a mapping job that he helped me get, and which put me in debt for the first time in my life.

I was to map the agricultural disbursements within Northern Ontario, for which I needed a car ... hence the debt. Given the size of the area involved, I was either brave or stupid, but truthfully there was not a lot of agriculture taking place outside the clay belts. The project was delayed, hence not paid, and I had debt, which I was not accustomed to, although someone told me that debt was a fact of life in Canada ... like an inheritance.

When the Department Head did not appreciate that I had picked up a part-time, early am position (six to nine am) tracing radioactive particles in a nuclear reactor department to pay for my car, I quit and took the next teaching job advertised. This I could do thanks to my Landed Immigrant status, an obvious step along the scenic route.

The University had been an eye-opening experience, and it is probably true that I and my friends, all expats, were a wee bit arrogant in our initial approach to "frosh", who we referred to as Grade X1V. We had individual rooms on the first floor of the male residence, and were there to work, graduate and move on. We were not interested in Hall activities or petty rules and regulations, and we certainly had no intention of attending meetings. I was fined a number of times for nonattendance, and I had to write "bollocks" a few times on notices and place them back in the student president's mailbox. Eventually he got the message.

Needless to say I didn't make many undergraduate friends. Most Saturday evenings, we would play cards and then wend our way to Paddy Green's Tavern for the "sawdust experience". The conversations were largely political and international in nature. The Cuban Crisis was a case in point. We were shocked that the undergrads were excited and in favour of the blockade. We worried that one side would go too far and push the nuclear button. We felt like lost souls surrounded by warmongers, and we knew that Canadian ships were part of the blockade

**The "little Englishman" and sister in school uniform.
In Formal Education**

(which the students did not). Any argument led to a "commie sympathizer" retort. We despaired.

One Saturday we left Paddy Green's earlier than usual and when we reached the campus there was music coming from the Student Union Building. Curiosity overcame us, and we went in. There was a live band and young people were dancing together. Remember that? It was when partners held each other and moved horizontally around the floor, slowly/closely or quickly depending on the tempo.

Apparently as we, six guys, entered the hall, they had announced a "Ladies Choice" and we were snapped up as fresh "meat." The young lady that I was dancing with was rather lovely and kept smiling at me in, I thought, a most becoming way. We continued together for the rest of the evening and I walked her to her residence. I later discovered that the reason for the smile was simply that she loved my accent and didn't understand a word that I said.

For a while I became her grad student. She was of German descent and was born in Ukraine, exiting with her family when Hitler retreated in 1944. I found all this very interesting, and even more so when her grandmother took an interest in me and baked all sorts of "goodies" for me, whenever she went home on weekends. I am not sure that putting on weight was a step in the right direction, but I find it a little coincidental that much later in my journey I should have two assignments in Ukraine, and that I currently have a Ukrainian family as guests in my home escaping Putin and the Russian invasion.

Chapter VII

Adventures in Public Education

Goderich, Ontario, where I began my career in Education was an enigma to me. First of all, it was a dry town, which I had never heard off, although the legion was licensed. Was there such a thing as a dry legion and the golf course on the edge of town had a license. Given what teachers were paid "a buck a beer" at the golf course was out of the question. My friend David, a Welshman and former Captain in British Intelligence, with a powerful thirst favoured the 15 cents a draft and the snooker table at the legion. This activity was frowned upon by some of Goderich finest and rumors were rampant, but there was another significant benefit. I used to drop into the legion after I had finished coaching (soccer and cross-country) the sons of Goderich finest. Since David and I were always there, well five days a week, we were part of the furniture, so to speak ... an institution.

The legion catered to many functions, and we became "best mates" to the delivery guys,resulting in a steady supply of wholesale cuts of beef, chicken, and pork. My friends had a large family while I was single, but it was like manna from heaven nonetheless. We ate and drank well in our two years in Goderich and I continued on the scenic route.

Speaking of scenery, Goderich is a very pretty town with a weird town layout. The Courthouse is at the town centre surrounded by a one way ring road with the other roads radiating out from the centre. However, the town was located along the shoreline of Lake Huron, which somewhat stunted the development of all roads leading westward. Another British screw-up?

Adventures in Public Education

    The story is that someone drew up plans for both Goderich and Galt, an inland town, and somehow the plans were switched. ???? You would think that someone would have had the gumption to notice that Goderich's western roads didn't go anywhere. After that mistake, perhaps that's why the Town Fathers declared a ban on alcohol consumption.

    I cannot say enough about my accommodation just north of the town. I had placed an ad in the local paper for a rental apartment for a single new teacher at the local high school. The response was somewhat underwhelming. Nothing good, and then I received a scruffy note written in shaky penmanship and unsigned, which stated that I should inquire at Ridgewood Park about the vacant apartment and listed a phone number.

    I duly called and spoke to a pleasant lady, who indeed, had an apartment to rent. Ridgewood Park was an estate surrounding a Georgian Cottage/mansion built for a former Bishop of the Arctic.

    Has the church come back to haunt me? Far from it, as I rented a huge one-bedroom apartment with an enormous living room, an eat-in kitchen, completely furnished in period furniture, carpeted, free parking, maid service every Thursday, all for $90.00 a month. Now it was over 60 years ago, however it was unreal and with a private estate and beach to boot.

    Things on this journey were looking up. Luxurious though my apartment may have been, there was very little that a small, Ontario town had to offer a 23-year-old Irishman in the prime of life. Most female potential company had left home after High School or else were wrapped up in the arms of a former school attachment.

    Many weekends I left to visit my friends in Hamilton, Ontario, about two to three hours away. It was on one of

Adventures in Public Education

these trips that I had my first introduction to the Canadian phenomenon known as winter driving. Normally it was a straight forward drive on Highway Eight, but one Sunday in November it started to snow upon leaving the town of Kitchener. The flakes were noticeably fluffy and large, and I felt a certain trepidation. By the time I reached the next sizeable town there was about 30 cm on the ground, and the windshield wipers on my 1958 VW Bug were having trouble clearing the volume. Furthermore, the windshield heaters on those early vehicles were not memorable in terms of efficiency.

Driving became a struggle, and if there had been a motel open, I would have pulled over. Everything was locked up tighter than a gnat's chuff.

At one point a snowplow came past me from the opposite direction and I thought I would be clever and cross over to the other side and drive on the cleared portion. The road was straight, with no curves or hills, and there was no traffic. Everyone but me had heard the weather forecast.

I eased over to the other side. What could go wrong? OOPs. My rear wheels were where all the weight was located in a VW Bug. I skidded on a patch of exposed ice and my car swept to the left onto the gravel verge. The tires dug into the dirt, and all of a sudden my front end was facing skyward, my rear end was digging in, and I was on the launch pad for a space orbit five years before the moon landings. It was a chilling experience which ended as quickly as it began when my trusty steed threw me back on the road.

I eased gently over to the correct lane and white knuckled it onward to Goderich. But that is not the end of the story.

I continued gingerly on my way through small towns and hamlets and to paraphrase Dickens "not a creature was stirring, but perhaps for some mice under the multiple centimetres of snow."

Several hours later I edged my way through the town of Goderich, crossed the bridge over the Maitland river and took the first left to Ridgewood Park. The road led me past the open space of the local airfield.

The falling snow was now coming at me horizontally, and I lost complete control and slid down into the ditch—expletives galore.

I forced my way out of the car, grabbed my overnight bag and struggled through the knee-high snow to the main house and the shelter of my apartment.

I was awakened out of a deep sleep at 6:30 in the morning by the telephone ringing. Of course the phone was not in my bedroom. After banging my toes on a hovering chair, I made it into the living room, accompanied by many expletives, to hear my landlady's voice inquiring as to the state of my health, given the terrible storm and the fact that my car was nowhere to be seen ... quite literally. I explained to her that I was fine but that my car was buried in the ditch somewhere off the road about 100 metres from her main gate. After commiserating with me, she told me that she would have the groundsman, Jack, get the estate tractor and help me find the car.

Some 40 minutes later, Jack and I emerged through the main gate with me standing on the back of the tractor holding a 10-foot pole. The car was nowhere in sight, only an undulating sea of white somewhat reminiscent of the surface of a lemon meringue pie. Jack continued along where he knew that the road had been, and I thrust the pole every tractor length into the snow, until ... THUNK! I found it.

We cleared the snow from around the car, attached a chain to the frame, and pulled it out. The trusty VW started right away. The TV ad was correct, this was a vehicle that the snowplow driver could use to get to the plow provided, of course, there were no ditches at the side of the road. Truly a bit of a glitch on my scenic route. But that is not the final winter snow story.

The following November, now a happily married man (after a whirlwind Montreal romance and engaged after the fourth date) I am back in Goderich. I had thought seriously of leaving Goderich after year one, but with an upcoming marriage I decided to stay on given my accommodation in the "BIG HOUSE" and the private estate.

Unfortunately the housing issue became complicated, and my wife and I moved into town and into the second floor of a senior lady's home.

Then the snow returned with a vengeance. There was so much snow blown up against our front door that I could not get out. I had to return upstairs, open the bedroom window, slide onto the roof of the front porch, and then jump into the snow covered garden. Then I retrieved a spade from the garage and dug my way to the steps, and exposed the front door.

That, however, was not the end of snowmageddon. That same evening, while returning from dinner at a friend's house on a neighbouring street, we were behaving like young newly-weds, you know, nudging one another, flicking snow at each other, and I gave her a gentle push. She went flying into a huge bank of snow and disappeared. "Oh my God," I exclaimed, as I furtively dug in the snow with my hands to find her. "I just married her, and now I've killed her."

When I finally gently brushed the snow from her face, I was surprised to find that she was laughing hysterically. I was sure then, although I never had doubts, that we had made the right decision to share our journeys as best friends and lovers.

Although I am enjoying my retirement life in a small Ontario community, it was not the right option at that early stage in our shared lives. My wife, who had grown up in Montreal, was uncomfortable being stared at and the subject of rumours. The funniest rumour actually was widespread before our marriage. A town matriarch may have started it by telling her granddaughter, who was also a student of mine, that I couldn't be getting married as I had a wife and 4 children living in Dublin, Ireland. Given that I was 23 at the time that would have been quite the feat.

I of course had never met or spoken to the matriarch. There was a more important reason for leaving Goderich, and that was embedded in Goderich's District Collegiate Institute. It was my first school teaching position, and it is hard to imagine a nicer, quieter, better-behaved student body. Forty per cent were farm kids, who all had work chores as part of life, and whose parents expected them to do well at school. The town kids were the usual mix with a few troublemakers, but nothing I couldn't handle.

A troubled area for me was the Grade-nine Initiation/Hazing, which I abhorred. The Physical Education Departments loved it, which says a lot about the games-mentality existing at the time, but for me, it was an excuse for bullying and embarrassing defenceless new members of the student body. I strenuously strove to stop any incident that I felt was out of line and thereby gained my second nickname. Remember as the "flying winger" at school I became "Leo", and as a first year teacher and "defender of the Innocent", I was known as "Old Roarsee". I have never been able to tolerate any sign of injustice, and thus laid down a marker for my journey.

Adventures in Public Education

The main problem area for me was the behaviour of the Camp Commandant (CC), who behaved more like an SS Officer than a high School Principal. Given the nature of the student body, he was way out of line. Apparently a few years before my arrival the school janitor had been fired for supplying members of the Senior Boys Football Team with beer after practice. It seemed to be an inappropriate gesture as it was not only improper but illegal and offended adults, especially in a dry town. Some students thought otherwise and organized a protest and marched out of school and up to the town centre and around the central circle, chanting and carrying protest signs. This must have alarmed some members of the community.

I am reminded of a stunt that my First XV rugby team pulled back in Ireland. We had a game in Newtonards, which required travel by public bus. After the game the hosts arranged for lunch in a local *café*, and then we took the bus back to Belfast. We missed a bus and had to wait another hour, and the English teacher accompanying us, in the absence of the coach, asked us what Mr. Evans would normally do in these circumstances? We lied and told him that Mr. Evans would normally buy us a pint. He thought that was a good idea, and WE TROUNCED OFF TO A LOCAL PUB where "Bunny" picked up the tab. A good day with a rugby victory, and a pint, and the only casualty was a somewhat red-faced English teacher in school the following week. A good prank, and we never heard a word in retribution.

Not so in Goderich ... such behaviour was too much for the School Board. The current Principal was eased into early retirement and a search was begun for a stern replacement to restore order ... hence the Camp Commandant. Problem was that by the time my Welsh friend, Head of Moderns, and I arrived, there was no disorder to sort out. We found the atmosphere somewhat stifling and neither of us liked to be ordered around. Control/order was the name of the game.

The CC, with a gimpy leg, could walk around the school in three minutes. Therefore, students were given three minutes to change classes. To ensure the regularity of this, the CC would stop whatever he was doing when the bell rang and gimp around the school. Malingerers were sent to the office for disciplining/detention.

All staff, no matter what they were doing, had to move to the centre of the hallway and ensure all traffic moved swiftly. You could not address a student question or concern when the bell rang. When he passed you he would give you a wee nod with his head. As he sped past me and down the hall he had to make a sharp right, just before reaching my friend, David. Quite often he and I would turn to face each other and give a full British military salute before re-entering our classrooms.

Amongst other actions, the CC appointed our Federation representative, and no one complained. I was too inexperienced to realize that our Rep should have been voted in by the staff, and I did have a run-in with our Rep, Jack, which resulted in Eileen and me picking up stakes and moving outta there.

In the Spring the CC decided that there needed to be a career's night for parents. In his divine wisdom, he decided that it would be held on a Friday evening. Now I ask you: student dances are held on Fridays and some staff volunteer their time, but an evening with parents? ... unheard of. On a Monday – Thursday ... OK, but on a Friday ... never ... and to not be asked. It was an order. Staff were expected to attend. There was no way I would attend even if I had a previous engagement.

Adventures in Public Education

At that time I was playing rugby for Toronto Irish and I had a game in Peterborough on Saturday afternoon. There was no way I was driving from Goderich on a Saturday to Peterborough and then playing a game. I told Jack, the Rep who had been appointed as the careers organizer, that he had better find a replacement as I would not be there. Later that day, I received a note from the High Command stating that I was expected at school. It was like a red flag to a bull, and I reminded the Rep that he had better find a replacement.

When I returned to school on Monday there was a note in my mailbox ordering me to see the SS CC during my only spare period of the day. In those days one only had three a week. I showed up, but my tail was not between my legs. Quite the opposite, an injustice had occurred, and I was ready for a fight.

He opened up with a tirade as to how I had gone down in his estimation as exemplified by my recent behaviour. I promptly laughed at him and told him that he had never been high in mine. I reminded him that in my own time I coached soccer, track and field, and cross-country running. In addition, I had organized the school's first ever overnight Geography Field-trip to Industrial Hamilton, the Niagara Escarpment, the Niagara Fruit belt, and Niagara Falls. This had taken up a lot of my personal time. I then stated that I had contributed more than most to the successful operation of the school, but my personal time is mine to give and could not be allocated by others. I left the room.

The following Friday, Eileen and I left for the massive teacher hiring frenzy at the Park Plaza Hotel in Toronto. I came away as the new Assistant Head of Geography for a school in Brampton, working for a true gentleman Principal.

Adventures in Public Education

The following Monday it felt great handing in my letter of resignation, and my Welsh friend picked up another Headship in a nearby town. As things worked out, my journey was going onward and upwards, and I seemed to be leaving some fools in my wake.

I heard that the CC was later replaced by the History Head, who was a reasonable guy.

Chapter VIII

Career Advancement

The next year is a bit of a blur. We found a great 2 BR apartment on the top floor of 6000 Yonge Street and I made the daily trip along HW 7, then a country road, where I could buy eggs from a Polish smallholder.

The most remarkable thing occurred one November evening when I was driving towards Toronto, and suddenly it disappeared ... The big power failure stretched all the way to New York and Boston ... Eighteen-floors is a brave climb, culminating in an apt with no power. Guess what we did that evening along with thousands of other desperate souls?

In the USA the maternity wards were busy some nine months later, but not in Canada, as we are such a refined group, and practice birth control.

On the education front I was introduced to the joys of Outdoor Education and the real impact of experiential learning, where every action had an immediate impact, real meaning, and gratification. Given that most activities were performed in teams, they reinforced communication and leadership skills and we, as instructors, learnt how to ensure that all were involved.

Despite being away from Eileen, I was always invigorated by my weekends spent at the Metro Conservation Authority's Schools, and my journey might easily have veered in a different direction. As it was, field trips were an important part of my work in the 25 years I was associated with schools. I believe that these events were extremely successful, so much so, in one case a student's father, a CEO of a company, offered me a bus to be used by the school. Unfortunately I did not have

Career Advancement

permission to accept the offer because, in the interests of equality, every school would have to have a bus.

By the end of the year in Brampton, I was on the move again ... onward and upward. My colleague, Don, was motivated to become an administrator/VP at a new school opening up nearby, and my Principal offered me the Headship, should he succeed. He did not, and I thought that if my current Principal thought that I was Headship material with three-years experience, someone else might. Plus I was driving quite a distance each day, and we were expecting our first child. Into the fray I went once more, and I emerged the new Geography Department Head at a brand new North York Secondary School, 30 minutes from home. In addition, as a new secondary school I had a very nice budget to equip the department with the tools of my trade.

Shaken by the appearance of Sputnik in the overhead sky, the Canadian Government had decided to fund secondary education in which technical subjects were taught. We benefited from the largess.

The next two years were a whirlwind. Outdoor Education continued with the creation of a Geography Club and weekend programs at the Conservation Areas. I did not want the repeat of an incident that occurred when I was in Brampton, where a young lady, brought up in an apartment, fainted when she saw a cow in a field adjacent to a Conservation Area. Students needed more exposure to the great outdoors, and this is probably even more important today in our techie world. They also needed to understand the complexities of the Built Environment, and we had students carrying out traffic surveys and analyzing the data.

We took students to Montreal to learn the intricacies involved in the functioning of a major port, intertwined with multiculturalism. I organized a French program in Montreal for the French department, which included a day

Career Advancement

hosted by Steinberg's grocery chain, in which the chain explained how one operated in a bilingual market amidst strong cultural differences, including food tastes, advertising, etc.

I continued coaching track and field and in doing so enacted one of my classic ruses. One of the students was very, very fast. In California, he had been a Junior 100 m Olympian. Since I had also been a sprinter, the students kept egging me on to have a race with him. I don't think I'm stupid, and I was old (26), hadn't raced in years, and with a six-month-old daughter, not necessarily getting a full night's sleep ... so I resisted the challenge, but only for so long. I knew that I had to yield, but I also knew that I had to avoid humiliation.

On the fateful afternoon we both lined up at the start. A student acted as starter and on the gun I threw everything I had into the start. WE WERE TIED and I pulled up holding my thigh after about three metres. Because of my age the assembled body believed my yarn of a thigh strain, and honour upheld, I continued coaching.

That story is almost as good as when my stomach was upset, and I walked through a crowd of students quietly farting and laughing when they were arguing amongst themselves as to who had dealt it.

There were so many things going on and along with new parenting the times they were confusing. This leg of the journey had many opportunities. I was a consultant with a Canadian publisher, and they were talking about a book. I was on the board's Outdoor Education committee, and the Superintendent wanted me to attend a summer program at the University of Vermont to become the Secondary Panel's outdoor ed "expert." I had an interview at Ryerson for a position teaching Urban Geography. This was at the behest of the father of one of my students, and finally, out of the blue, Eileen and I received an appointment for a

Career Advancement

Canadian International Development Agency(CIDA) interview for an overseas teaching position. I say "out of the blue" because I do not remember applying to CIDA, but I must have done. As to why, God only knows ... wanderlust? ... extend the journey globally? ... dissatisfaction with my current position? ... definitely not —after all, according to some, I was working in an educational paradise.

Well, guess who won out? Eileen did. At the interview we were asked as to where we would like to be posted. I said East Africa, which is a region of the world I had been fascinated with for some time. Eileen said Trinidad and Tobago. After we left the room, I asked her why she said Trinidad, as we had never talked about a placement. She replied that she had met someone from there ONCE.

Weeks later we received a call from a moving company asking if they could have the contract to move us to TRINIDAD. This was before our official offer, so someone's palms were crossed with silver on the sly. A few days later we received the official invitation to be part of the International Assistance Program to Trinidad and Tobago. My assignment was to establish an A level program in Geography at St George's College, Barataria, Trinidad.

What to do? Three possible career/adventure assignments and a young family to boot. What to do? We talked and talked, and to be honest, my beloved was game for anything. She always was much braver than me, although I did join her on a hot air ballooning trip. But she snorkelled among the barracuda in Tobago, and went up in a glider near Ottawa.

We opted to continue the scenic voyage and go to Trinidad. Some people thought that we were crazy, and maybe we were, but loveable and lovingly crazy, especially

Career Advancement

as Eileen had discovered that we were expecting our second child a few months before the offer.

In reality, we were expanding the scenic route to parts previously unknown to us ... who else amongst our friends has spent Simon Bolivar's birthday in Ciudad Bolivar on the Orinoco River in Venezuela? But more on that later.

The die was cast. The journey was on.

Chapter IX

The Caribbean

The beauty of a corporate or government move is that you don't have to do much, The movers do it all. You simply have to have lots of three-coloured tape, one colour for storage, one for Trinidad, and one for a third destination, in this case my in-laws where we would spend some months before the move. In our case this was complicated as Eileen was due to deliver in August and the departure date was also August.

The most horrible experience was our visit to Toronto General for our tropical shots, the worst of which was Typhoid, Paratyphoid, and Tetanus. Wow, did your arm hurt after that? It was the worst ever. Apparently in the military after they administer that shot, they take you to the parade ground and march you for an hour and that eases the pain. We, however, had to go home as a newborn required his mother.

Try holding a newborn with a painful, aching arm. The rest was a breeze, sort of ...

Only a National government agency would book you on a Vanguard on a flight to Trinidad from Toronto, with stops in Montreal, Bermuda, Bahamas, Antigua. Barbados and Trinidad. The Vanguard was a turboprop aircraft ... Hey, government, haven't you heard of jet aircraft? ... Maybe the bureaucrats didn't care, as Air Canada was the only airline flying turboprops into the Caribbean.

To make matters worse, one poor child, Eric, had ear trouble, and effectively cried for much of the trip.

There were six of us, plus families going to Trinidad. Eileen and the two children, including our newborn son, stayed behind for six-weeks. Through an acquaintance, I

The Caribbean

had met one of the participants before leaving Canada. In fact, we had researched the need to purchase an imported car from Ford, UK, to be delivered in Port of Spain. We had duty-free status as semi "diplomats". Our early collaboration meant that I was not alone on the new journey, and I appreciated that.

<u>The Tropics</u>

Hot ... Humid ... Lush ... Luxuriant ... Steamy ... Stifling ... Sultry ... Sweltering ...

The tropical air is quite distinctive, especially in the wet season. There is a certain succulence in the air that you can taste. There are a rich variety of flavours that you can also taste. It is all very unique and almost overwhelming. However, after ten hours in a Vanguard, also overwhelming, I had two quick rums and hit the sack in the Bretton Hall Hotel, Port of Spain. I was instantly asleep. Thankfully, the Cicadas heavenly crescendo does not reach until noon, and I was able to sleep in until 9:00 am, thereby missing what became for me the best time of the day, the early morning, when the air is fresh and cool.

Settling into the routines of a new country has its challenges. We did not have to locate homes, as the TT Government did that. However, that's where it became interesting. Apparently UNESCO covered our housing and previous participants had been allocated a sum of money every month for rent. As a result they found some really nice homes and were very comfortable.

In our case we were allocated government housing, built originally by the British Colonial Office, and the deal was not as good. Did someone pocket my rental allowance, while I shared a semi-detached dwelling with a Hindu, alcoholic, eye doctor and his family, working as a psychologist in the nearby mental hospital? I am not sure when he worked, as his part of the building was

The Caribbean

continuously visited by a veritable cross-section of Port of Spain's alcoholics. His wife only knew one song, sorry, four lines of one song, and she repeated them day and night, week after week, month after month, until one eventually became immune.

<u>Que sera, sera</u>

>Whatever will be, will be,
>The futures not ours to see, to see,
>Que sera, sera

I tried to move, especially when it came to our attention that Deo was telling people that he had been intimate with Eileen and was providing his drinking cronies with mythical descriptions of her body. The TT Ministry of education, to whom I had been assigned, was not particularly sympathetic and showed me an empty house in the middle of nowhere, which we declined. We rationalized that Deo was not in his right mind most days, and no one would believe that Eileen could even contemplate such an incident occurring.

Que sera, sera.

Now that the housing was sorted, it was time to check out my employment and also visit Maracas Beach, located on the other side of the Northern Mountain Range. The Cortina GT that I had ordered from Dagenham in England was still there. The supply chain had been disrupted by a strike at a battery plant, so I went back to my roots and rented a 1968 VW BUG. This was a much more refined model than my 1958, almost a space monster, and fun to drive.

First things first, let's sort out the work situation. I drove, with my new Trinny driving license, to St. George's College, Barataria. I had been assigned to St George's in order to establish an A level Geography program. A-levels are University entrance exams based on the UK system, but now administered within the former British West Indies.

To my surprise, the Headmaster did not want the program, as he was blinded by Maths and Latin. He was happy for me to fill in a geography slot in his timetable. What to do? Do I phone up CIDA and tell them I wasn't really needed, and maybe I should go home ... and interrupt the passage along the scenic route, or say "screw it, I am in the Caribbean, my Canadian stuff is in storage, I can do the job blindfolded, giving us time to go to the beach, party, watch first class cricket, try new foods and maybe travel to South America?"

Venezuela was visible from south-west Trinidad. Guess what, the scenic journey continued next to the beach. At the hotel I had met Leroy, a Trinny pharmaceutical sales representative. This has to be distinguished from a Trinny drug sales person: individuals who are somewhat prevalent nowadays and responsible for the current, 2025, State of Emergency and the murder totals of over 600 people annually. He was single and seemed to have a second career shepherding tourists around the sights, the pan yards and restaurant/bars, etc. He probably earned something from places he visited, not the least would be free drinks.

With us, it was a different situation, as we were there for at least two years and not a casual visit. Our relationship was mutually beneficial, as he would drop in for meals and we would get medicines from him. He took me for my first visit to Maracas Beach and my first Caribbean Sea bath ... warm salty water ... lovely. Afterwards we went to his favourite Chinese restaurant, where we were spoiled, and the meal was on the house. Of course, we visited the restaurant a lot as paying customers over the coming years.

The Caribbean

Two sculptured Heads by Artists, Fernandez and Hernendez, who lived in communities in the Northern Coastal Range in Trinidad.

The Caribbean

But back to the beach. Have you tried gin in coconut water from a freshly cut coconut? That was my first drink on a tropical beach provided by a generous Trinny Indian family, who seemed pleased to have a Canadian newbie on the beach beside them. I must admit that it is an acquired taste, like my first avocado from our garden tree, or my first guava, also from the garden. I seem to prefer my gin the old, colonial way with lemon/lime and tonic water.

Beside the "eye candy", both male and female (at that time there were only two genders), another beach delight was surfing. I only body surfed, but in the next two years, I lived in body surfing heaven at Maracas, Togo, Mayaro, and others. Sunday and holidays were our go-to beach days.

I have never lived in a place with so many holidays. Thanks to the nature of Trinidad as a multicultural nation, we celebrated Christian holidays, Hindu holidays, Muslim Holidays, Carnival, May the First (International Labour Day), and assorted cricket days.

Eileen was a strong swimmer and loved to snorkel, especially on the sister island of Tobago. At the Arnos Vale shallow reef she swam with stingrays and barracuda, while I preferred the glass bottomed boat at Buccoo Reef and the Nylon Pool. Who would argue that we weren't on a scenic route?

While on the beach, I had an early introduction to the workings of the capitalist system (not to be confused with Prime Minister Eric Williams' impressive tome on capitalism and slavery).

My friend John and I had gone to a Bay Street, Toronto, Ford Dealership and ordered two new vehicles from Ford UK, (right-hand drive) as we were permitted to bring a duty-free car for our assignments He had a large family and so ordered a Ford Station wagon, while I with a young family ordered a two-door Ford GT Cortina with a souped

The Caribbean

up engine, sports gears, a beige interior in British RACING GREEN.

My car was held up by strike action in a battery plant and was delayed about six weeks while John's was delayed only a few weeks. I was receiving regular telegrams from Ford telling me about my car and I eagerly traced its passage across the Caribbean. The morning the ship docked I was at the Ford dealers at dawn to return my rental and give them the necessary documents to retrieve my GT from Customs. I even waited for it to be delivered, plated, then drive away in my WHITE GT CORTINA WITH A BLACK INTERIOR. What can you do? You can't send it back even with a black interior in the tropics.

The following Sunday at our weekly pilgrimage to the beach, John and I compared our new cars and I noticed several things. "John," I said, you have a different battery than I have. In fact your battery is from here, while mine says UK." Upon closer examination, we discovered that his tyres were Trinidad made Dunlops, while mine were made in the UK. His car had been at the dealers for a few days and someone had swapped those parts for "buy local" products. My vehicle had barely been at the dealers, and I was there. The Trinidad government to encourage the development of manufacturing, absent in the colonial economy, had given certain companies the exclusive rights to produce certain commodities, and they did, without competition ... and of an inferior quality, hence the swap.

Carnival

One cannot argue that the highlight of the Trinny year is MAS or CARNIVAL. Sometimes it might be argued that elements of the populace go overboard in their preparation for this annual display of bacchanal. People have been

The Caribbean

known to make personal and family sacrifices to raise the cash to play in a band.

The season itself begins after Xmas and ends with the onset of Lent, but the big bands start preparations during the previous Lent. What is a band, you might ask? A band comprises a group of people, numbering from hundreds to over a thousand, who join together under a band leader. The band leader provides the vision and artistic flow to create an annual masterpiece of floats, costumes, etc. around a differing theme each year.

The colours are magnificent and the music from steel bands and brass bands is infectious. The most audacious costumes are reserved for the King and Queen of the band, and their places cost the participants thousands.

There is also a cheap Mas in which the customers are much less expensive. "Sailor" is a common cheap version in which the participants are dressed as Yankee sailors. Eileen and I played cheap Mas with CIBC Starlift, in which we were dressed in Red (men) and Yellow (women) boiler suits, as mechanics carrying huge, wooden wrenches. This was on Carnival Monday, with the main event on Tuesday for which we had Grandstand tickets.

Boiler suits on a hot day may not seem like a great idea to you, and you would be right, but the suits had many pockets for mickeys of rum or water ... your choice. The costume did lead to a specific event that occurred because I was slightly looped. I was able to use the event many years later in an attempt to endear myself to a Trinny audience when my close Trinny friend (who was paying for the wedding) asked me to act as the MC, where Eileen and I stood out as the only white people in the room.

The Trinny incident occurred when Starlift was winding its way along the parade route in Port o Spain, making many stops on route. This was a big parade, with multiple

The Caribbean

bands and musicians. We were accompanied by the Starlift Steel Band, and it was hot.

On the sidewalk I spotted three young people drinking water from a new steel bucket. There were two girls and a guy, all in their early 20s. I went over and asked one of the girls if she could spare some water for a cousin. She replied that if I was a cousin of hers something was pretty strange. I then asked her if she had never heard of the "BLACK IRISH"? Upon which she emptied the remaining water over me ... thus baptizing me in Trinidad, and later helping me raise laughter from a group of wedding guests.

The delights of carnival stretch far beyond the events of Monday/Tuesday. There are large *Fêtes* with dancing and drinking, house parties, calypso competition, pan contests, old Mas, and King/Queen contests. There is much prestige to be gained from being Calypso King/Queen or being Band King/Queen.

Pick pockets were everywhere, and our cash was always in Eileen's bra. We figured that she would notice if some foreign hands attempted to retrieve it. I must admit that it was somewhat humorous, when we were with four couples at our first large *fête*, and the husbands all reached their hand towards the wives, and they automatically placed their hands inside their Bras.

***

Eileen's Voice on Mas and living in Trinidad:

Have you ever noticed that when you pass someone on the street that they stare at you? Probably not—you are a part of the community around you—therefore a member of the tribe. This has nothing to do with ethnicity or colour. You fit into the faceless mass, comfortable in your city and well versed in its ways.

I had found that shopping in Port of Spain always left me with a real sense of being a stranger. I imagined that people were looking at me as if to say "You are not from here," and I felt discomfort with my "otherness". This had nothing to do with the colour of my skin, as the Trinidadian population is reflective of all the various influences of its colonial past; Spanish, French Portuguese, English, etc.

Our first carnival season was met with excitement and a certain amount of trepidation. Our first *fête* of the season was the annual People's National Movement (PNM), the ruling party, carnival *fête* held at the Oval, the national cricket ground. Lots of music, steel bands and brass bands were pouring their offerings of the new calypsos with so much power, the ground trembled.

Around the perimeter were the food vendors selling everything from fish (shark and bake) to roti, pelau, spiced peanuts and dried chana to beer and rum punch. It was a night to remember. Eric Williams, the Prime Minister and his cabinet were there and, obviously, security forces from the mounted division of the police service were there to keep an eye on things.

As the evening progressed, lots of drinks were consumed and relief was needed. We headed to the port-a-potties, and spied the most beautiful horse, who was sat upon by a police man, who would have looked official if it weren't for the large glass of booze in his hand. It should be pointed out that this police detail near the toilets was well hidden from the official PNM party, and we know that "royalty" does not need a public washroom.

While stroking the patient horse, we asked him for the horse's name. "Kildare, and he is Canadian bred" was the reply. An Irish name on a Canadian horse ... an instant love affair, but we had other urgencies to deal with. We went back to our friends with a new story to tell.

The party continued. An Irish friend, Liam Shanigan, got very drunk but sobered up instantly, when we noticed that his wife, Emer, was being led to an exit by a man she

The Caribbean

had been dancing with. In due course, another trip was made to the right side of the grounds. I'm pretty sure it was to see our new friend and his rider again. We felt an affinity towards this mounted police office, although later he told us that he was a bit frustrated as we were cutting into his drinking time.

The phone rang, a racket causing severe pain to my hung over head. I answered and heard a mumble, which I didn't understand. The accent was so strong that I had to listen very intently, not an easy feat with an addled brain. " Tyson here, from last night. Do you remember? We are having a small party at my house on Monday night. Just a few friends and we were wondering if you would like to experience a local event."

I was having real trouble with his accent and had to repeat the invitation to be sure that I understood him.

We arrived at his house, where there were six men sitting in the porch and the women were inside. Herbert introduced me to his wife Nola, who welcomed me into the company of women. Tom was given a drink and went to join the men. Our experiences were very different: the women were curious about my children, what kind of food I cooked, had I eaten traditional food like pelau, the ubiquitous carnival dish or cook up. I was eager to learn the local cuisine and felt really comfortable with my new friends.

Tom, on the other hand, was met with suspicion by the brotherhood. What was the white man doing here? Was he slumming? Why was he not at the Officers Mess? What were his motives? These same men were there for the party when we left, and they did not want us to leave ... friends and comrades with two years of shared experiences.

Herbert and Nola became our closest friends in Trinidad, and indeed friends for life, with visits back and forth.

***

The Caribbean

Like all things, Carnival seems to have changed, and I wonder if we did not experience the best of times. The last time we were in Trinidad much of the music was coming from gigantic BOOM BOXES where the emphasis is not so much on melody and rhythm but the BOOM. We, on the other hand, enjoyed the melodies and rhythms of sweet pan and the swinging sounds of brass. The music was non-stop and many years later I still have the discs and my hearing.

I wonder if today's generation will be able to say the same. The other big change has occurred in the scanty nature of costumes. There is not much to them these days. We used to say that with all the rum, which used to be really cheap, and the many *fêtes*, if one's marriage was on shaky ground before one moved to Trinidad, it would not survive. Happy days ... our journey continued.

On our return to Toronto, our sea shipment contained three base pans, two tenor pans, and a treble pans. The latter three came with stands, and all came from Pan Am North Stars, care of my friend, Herbert. There is a rumour that the base pans were turned upside down and had rum in them, but I can neither confirm or deny that, as I did not accompany the shipment.

After decorating our recreation room for many years, we donated the set to the Music Department of a Scarborough High School.

Life in Trinidad was very pleasant. Given our ages, 24 and 28, given that we had two young children, aged eight-weeks to two-years, we certainly were very active. The key was that due to the vast salary differences between Ontario and Trinidad, we could afford a live-in maid. In fact, it was expected that we did to support the local economy.

When I first moved into the house, I was inundated by people either looking for work or asking me to hire their sister or cousin or some other family member. Given that

The Caribbean

Eileen was bringing a baby to a very different country, culture, and environment, I thought that it was necessary.

I had to fire the first two employees for a number of reasons. I identified a personality trait, which I called the maid mentality, which we had trouble living with in the same house. This mentality came about from the way maids were treated by the employers. They were considered as a subservient species, poorly treated, poorly paid, and worked long hours with one day off every 14 days. If one had company, one would close the kitchen door so that the maid heard nothing, and you know that the first thing the maid would do was to place her ear at the keyhole, and then gossip the information with neighbouring servants. This resulted in an attitude difference between employers and employees that was difficult for us to live with due to our egalitarian belief.

So for a short while we lived without a live-in, and engaged instead a young woman as a cleaner on a part-time basis. Then we hit the jackpot. We needed a babysitter and our cleaner suggested her sister, and one thing led to another, and her sister, Judith, became our live-in. Jackpot you ask? Well Judith had never worked as a domestic, and had a great sense of pride. She had never been put down (except by her mother) and was very dependable. Her last job until being made redundant was in the Maidenform bra factory. She could be a handy contact at Carnival time!!!!!!!! We paid her double the local wage, and her evenings were free unless we needed a babysitter, and she had a one room plus bathroom unit behind the main house. She was happy and so were we.

We suggested that unless we had company, she would eat her dinner with us. The first time this was to happen I entered the dining area and the table had been set with us at one end and a lonely place at the far end of the table. I moved the outlier up to meet the rest and left the room.

The Caribbean

When I returned, the isolated setting had been moved halfway down the table, and I smiled and left it there. It was the start of a great friendship, which lasted beyond our life in Trinidad to her staying with us for a while in Toronto, until she moved to New York, and we lost touch.

Judith is responsible for one of my journey's embarrassing moments. She was pregnant when she came to work for us with her first child at 27 years of age. Seemed like a good age for us and, we had no problems, only her mother. We were able to work around her health issues, but Eileen's mother in Canada fell and broke her leg. She and the kids returned to Toronto and Judith and I soldiered on.

When delivery time arrived, I drove her to the hospital and went into the emergency department with her. I swear that everyone in the department stopped and stared at us. Later a Trinny TV personality enacted the scenario to me ... as follows:

"Eh. White man get she pregnant!!! He can't be all bad. He bring her to hospital."

Red face ... red face ... red face ... Where was my wife when I needed her ... Toronto.

STOP PRESS: Do you believe in coincidence? As I was typing this the TV was playing in another room. There was an Aussie TV program called Darby and Joan, and suddenly I heard a familiar singer playing in the background. It's Dusty Springfield, who was big when we were in Trinidad, and she is singing ...

"You don't have to say you love me just be close at hand ..."

I actually have that on a 45, and we used to listen to it in Trinidad 55 years ago, but not since.

Trinidad played an incredible role in our evolution. I met a man named Herbert Tyson, who was to become my life long best friend and his wife Nola who was Eileen's

The Caribbean

ivory to her steel. When they went shopping, this is how they referred to themselves. It was the title of an LP featuring Winnifred Attwell on the piano and Pan AM North Stars Steel band. I became aware for the first time in my life of the nature of Imperialism, Colonialism and Racism. This changed forever the way I viewed the world, and I was no longer the "little Englishman" created by my formal secondary education. I had a whole new world to study and research. I did both at the University of the West Indies and in Toronto. I read Capitalism and Slavery, the work of Eric Williams, the then Prime Minister of Trinidad and Tobago, the novels of V.S.Naipaul and Edgar Mittelholzer, and the Nigerian novelist and poet Chinua Achebe. A whole new Tom Lyons had emerged from this leg of my journey, and was so much richer for it.

I changed so much that my mother wanted to know if I was a communist, and I had to assure her that human rights, peace, a sustainable environment and equitable international development were not the mainstay of existing communism.

There was a super fun side to all of this which will never be forgotten. I have previously mentioned carnival and the myriad of activities associated with it during January-March. However, let's not forget the Indian weddings we were invited to. The rich wedding with an incredible display of wealth, complete with competing teams of drummers, elephants (not indigenous) and the brides-to-be multiple changes into ever more gorgeous saris.

The more normal wedding—in humble surroundings, no alcohol and the food was served up on banana leaves. One ate with one's hands and the hot mango peppers were stomach destroying. Both were fantastic experiences and enriched our journey.

Then there were our own house parties, never to be repeated in Canada. Mind you, at that time I was buying

The Caribbean

rum by the gallon for about $4.00 Can. Also, my circle of friends/acquaintances was wider in Port of Spain.

At our home *fêtes* we had some of my colleagues, a few Canadians (not too many, as we did not want to spoil the mood) teacher college students that I knew (an essential element as they were guaranteed to start dancing) local TV personalities such as Holly Betaudier, the West Indies Star cricket fast bowler, some journalists and writers, my police friends and a few selected neighbours, which included a police Superintendent, a judge, and several doctors, including Winston, the only heart surgeon on the island—a true gentleman and a good man to know.

The routine was very simple. It was not going to rain, so the heavy furniture was carried outside to the lawn. Chairs were placed against the walls. A small boom cabinet was hooked up against one wall. Our championship Weimaraner (granddaughter of a CRUFTS best of breed winner) was locked up in her large dog house.

I purchased a huge cured ham from a local Hi Lo supermarket and 100 hops bread (large rolls) from a neighbouring bakery. The hams and hops were not complete without my friend, Herbert's, sister-in-law Beaulah's pepper sauce made in Pepper Village in South Trinidad ... exquisite, there is no better word to describe it.

These events were truly memorable, but at my current age, either because of age or the rum or because they were so long ago, seem to me to be a bit of a blur.

Two events stand out. Unfortunately a Canadian friend met one of my work colleagues and started an affair at one of the Fêtes. His wife and kids were also our friends, and we felt bad and somewhat responsible, given that it began in our home. After the family split up, I apologized to Joan, and she graciously said that I had nothing to apologize for, because if it had not been my colleague it would have been someone else.

The Caribbean

The second incident involved Hilltop Wolf Fox Bluebonnet, our Weimaraner, called Snoopy by Kelly, our two-year-old. The largest group at these events were the students, and they were 25% males and 75% females, who loved to dance. After they had had two or so drinks, the girls would place their third drink under the chairs, and during the course of the evening, many would get knocked over.

After the last guests had left, Snoopy was let out of her house, as she patrolled the grounds in the evening, and we left her to her own devices. At 6:00 am when I opened the doors, Snoopy was lying on the vestibule floor with her front paws over her head, suffering the worst doggy-headache from rum and coke. As an aside, I never drink rum and coke, only rum and soda, and if the rum is good with a little water ... no headache.

But now for a moment of truth—We held quite a few parties, and Snoopy never repeated the doggy-hangover.

How many of you can honestly say that after the first hangover, you deliberately avoided another ... Be honest. There are humans who consider other animals as dumb.

I have said nothing about work as there was little to say. St Georges was straightforward, and the students did their work. There was a lot of family pressure to do well, and I felt sorry for them at times due to exam pressure. Remember that they started the pressure loaded system at 11/12-years-of-age. My Trinny colleague, Marilyn, and I added some outreach to enrich their experience. I chartered an ancient Vickers Viscount airplane from BWIA, sold seats to 40 students, and went for a junket around Trinidad for 90 minutes at between 1500-2000 feet. It was quite the ride. I stood in the cockpit between the pilot and copilot and pointed out the Trinny features out the window, totally oblivious as to conditions in the cabin.

The Caribbean

When we landed I had a surprise. Most of the students had never flown before and at lower elevations it can be quite bumpy, as a result a number, perhaps a lot, had been sick. That excursion was never repeated. We also went with a botanist/naturalist to the mangrove swamps of Caroni. This first-hand close up experience would later, in 2004, make me wonder how many of the roughly 230,000 lives lost as a result of the Indian Ocean tsunami, would have been saved, if the 14 countries affected had retained their coastal mangrove forests. I would bet on mangrove over water any time.

Chapter X

Excursion to Venezuela

One of the advantages of being located in Trinidad is that it makes a good jumping off point for trips to South America, and so we made several of those. In August of 1969, Eileen and I went to Venezuela. We had not been paying much attention to the international news and had forgotten that the first ever airplane bombing took place on a flight from Caracas, Venezuela to Cuba.

I have been curious about two things related to this act of terrorism. Firstly, despite the fact that the bomber ended up living in Florida, should we assume that the CIA were not involved, and secondly, if the first airplane bombing had not been covered by global media, would we have had a second attack?

This obviously had changed the way Venezuelans handled airport security. It was a bit shocking to us, when we walked down the steps from the plane, to see mounted on a flatbed truck, directly facing the steps, several soldiers with a machine gun aimed at the plane.

Because we travelled around on a DC-3 from airport to airport, we were thoroughly body searched; bags were searched. This was the first time we experienced this, and given what we knew, it actually was comforting. However, on one flight from Ciudad Bolivar, on the Orinoco River, we weren't searched. I started to panic, because we wanted to be searched.

We liked Venezuela. Caracas has a super climate, not too hot, not cold, and relatively dry. The food was fantastic. We ate many of our meals in Caracas at a small Café called "The Royal Quick Lunch". The steaks were unbelievable.

Excursion to Venezuela

Our stay in Venezuela was notable for two events and one observation, namely, when travelling in Spanish-speaking South America, never travel on Simon Bolivar's birthday ... Everything is locked up tighter than a gnat's chuff.

When we arrived at the airport at Ciudad Bolivar, we were surprised to see Amerindians in traditional attire carrying bows and arrows while getting off other planes. This was definitely a first.

We checked into a very large Hotel in the centre of town overlooking the river, and were surprised to find very few people about. Eileen was not feeling well as she had picked up a heavy cold somewhere, and I must admit I chastised her a little bit, because not only was it her birthday, but I was actually taking her in the footsteps of Sir Walter Raleigh. He had visited here in the 17th century. This was not a winning comment.

The Orinoco basin is very different from the coastal mountains and plains, and it's very humid, so we made our way back to the hotel to quench our thirst with a Venezuelan beer. In the lobby we had to pass four men who were having a heated argument. One was obviously American, and was at least six feet four inches tall, and the other three were Venezuelan Spanish speaking. The argument was in Spanish, and we had no idea what was being said.

We kept on going to the enormous bar/dance hall area, where there was one lonely bartender and us. We found our way to a table and were enjoying a cool one, when into the room strolled the gigantic Texan. He stopped at the bar and called out to us, and asked if he could bring us a drink. We acknowledged him and readily accepted his hospitality.

His name turned out to be Tex Palmer, and he had been a pilot during World War II. After the war was over, given that he had an unfortunate relationship with his father, he

Excursion to Venezuela

ended up in Venezuela rather than Texas. He tried to start an aviation company, but the Venezuelans kept refusing to give him a business license, so he flew for others. He proceeded to tell us that Venezuela had discovered a large alluvial Diamond deposit about 90 minutes away from where we were seated, and that he had flown in over a thousand miners to that site in a few months.

That explained the Amerindians at the airport. They were all going to be Diamond Diggers.

Tex proceeded to tell us that he wished he had a diamond to give us, but he had given them all away. He called the barman over and the barman took a handkerchief out of his pocket, opened it up, and inside was a good-sized, uncut diamond, sitting in an alluvial deposit. Tex then offered to fly us the next day to the diamond site, if the plane was flying. Apparently the argument he was having was with the mine owners, about the weight being carried on a flight the next day.

The plane, besides having the Amerindians we'd seen at the airport, was also carrying equipment, and even a jukebox and generator, and he felt there was too much weight.

Eileen would have been the only woman amongst over a thousand men, and although she could have made a fortune practising an ancient profession, it was not something that she thought of herself as doing. I certainly did not fancy my chances defending her honour against the bows and arrows of outrageous misfortune. We went to his room in the morning to tell him that we had decided to leave, and arrived as a waiter was bringing him breakfast. This was fortuitous, as Tex was out cold and the waiter had a key. On a bedside table was a huge wad of US hundred-dollar bills and an enormous pistol. We had truly arrived at the Wild West complete with Cowboys, bows and arrows, and "Indians."

Excursion to Venezuela

Before checking out, we went for a walk and found a small jeweller's shop where he showed some more of the new diamond find plus some Cochano Oro ... pure gold. We purchased some small bracelets made from pure gold, and I still have them.

Unfortunately being made from pure gold they were fragile, and broke.

We left the next day on our trusty DC-3 for the island of Margarita off the northwest coast of Venezuela. Margarita is also known as Pearl Island, and was part of Columbus's European discoveries in the 15th century. One of his infamous acts was to force Amerindian men to dive for pearls, which were found in abundance in this part of the Caribbean.

Today one can still buy pearls on Margarita, but where they come from is an open question. Eileen and I spent four or five days on the island; she basked in the Sun; I hid from the Sun, and then we went to the Pearl Houses.

These consisted of three or four very large Victorian style homes staffed by men, and in each room, besides chairs, there would be a series of small recessed tables, a bit like a billiard table with a felt covering, and no pockets. This is where the sellers opened bags and spread pearls on the covering.

The bags contained different colours, different sizes, and you could watch as they, with a gloved hand, moved the pearls around, while you decided what you wanted to buy.

We were getting a little low on cash, but we managed to buy about 30 pearls. However, at this stage of my life, I'm not sure where they've all gone. It was an interesting experience. Following that we left from Margarita for Caracas and Port of Spain.

It is interesting to note that there were a lot of Venezuelans in Port of Spain. Many of them were enrolled in English language schools to perfect their English. Our

Excursion to Venezuela

friend, Tex, had talked to us about sending his four kids to Port of Spain for boarding school, but alas, we never heard from him again.

About a month after we returned to Port of Spain, the Trinidad Guardian had a large morning headline; "VENEZUELAN GOVERNMENT ANNOUNCES HUGE DIAMOND DISCOVERY"

Chapter XI

Excursion to Suriname

In Suriname in 1921, a team of Aluminum Co of America (ALCOA) geologists came across a jungle tribe that was previously unknown, but to themselves. The government of the day tried to settle them in a fixed location with housing etc. This had gone on for about five or six months. Then, one morning when the government officials arrived at the camp, it was empty.

The tribe had decided that this life was not for them, and retreated back into the jungle, never to be seen or heard from until early 1969.

When I mentioned this to my friend, John, we wondered if we would be able to organize a trip to Suriname and visit with this community. We flew to Paramaribo, booked into a hotel, and went looking for a guide. At the hotel we met two American brothers and, over drinks, told them what we were up to. They wanted to come along and so the four of us hired a guide with a large canoe, a 40-horsepower Johnson, and two boys. I can't remember the guide's name. We will call him Joe. We negotiated the price and bought supplies for the trip. He would provide the camping gear.

We left Paramaribo for Albina on the Marowijne River. We were a bit nervous because we had left Trinidad before we had a chance to start taking anti-malaria medication. We bought quite a few boxes of mosquito coils to ward off the little critters.

Albina was an interesting historical town. On the French Guiana side was a prison link to the infamous Devil's Island offshore. This was a prison that was used largely for political prisoners from France. The prisoners were white, from France, and the prison guards were black, from Africa. Conditions were terrible, and although two ships a

Excursion to Suriname

year sailed from France to Albina with 100 prisoners a time, the prison was never full. Dysentery malaria, other diseases and physical abuse served to keep the prison population down. Nowadays just a series of empty buildings survive.

Our first night on the trip was actually quite comfortable, as we were the guests of a riverside convent. The next day we boarded the canoe and headed upriver.

The initial trip was uneventful. The jungle came right up to the water's edge and there was little evidence of wildlife. Every so often we came upon clearings with Bush Negro, now known as Maroons, villages The children would run along the water's edge and Joe would occasionally throw them treats.

The only visible sign of men consisted of old men or cripples. Joe explained that most of the men were working in the bauxite open pit mines in order to participate in the cash economy.

We did not stop at these early villages. Joe stated that they have tourist visitors and there is a tendency for the Maroons to put on a show, which they believe that tourists want to see but which is not related to real life.

We would make some stops further up the river. I have made the major theme of this book ... *my trip along the Scenic Journey of Life*. This is evidenced by examining the relatively temperate period that corresponded to my life in Ireland. The same can be said for the short period that I spent in Suriname. The Bush Negro, as I knew them, originated from escaped slaves originally brought by the English to their colony. At the end of the Seven Years War between the English and the Dutch, the peace treaty gave Suriname to the Dutch in exchange for New Amsterdam, which later became New York.

Excursion to Suriname

In the chaos ensuing during the handover period, as English plantation owners left, a large number of slaves found freedom by escaping inland into the jungle. There they established original West African societies far up river. They retained traditional agricultural practices, social habits, cultural traits, such as wood carving skills, of which I have a few pieces, and religious practices such as ancestor worship. Their villages were primarily on islands, and they practised tactics of guerilla warfare to protect themselves and in raiding plantations to free other slaves. They were very successful and successfully resisted all major European attempts to suppress them, despite or perhaps because of the Creole/white cruelty to those captured.

Welcomed by the children of the village

One simple technique was to place canoes strategically around their island homes, and when the invaders showed up at one end, they quietly paddled away and disappeared.

In the decades after our visit, things have become worse for the people now known as Maroons. Greed and the

Excursion to Suriname

Industrial World's thirst for timber and mineral resources have played havoc with the traditional rights of the indigenous Amerindians, and the Maroons. Things became worse after a military coup of the 80s. Legal "mambo-jumbo" backed up by modern weapons and aircraft destroyed villages, possibly some that I visited, and thousands of hectares of land were destroyed, flooded and decimated.

We Canadians think of ourselves as essentially well-meaning, generous, judicial people, but if you believe that, then you need to examine the activities of mining companies based in Montreal, Toronto and Vancouver, and the support they get from Canadian Governments, not only in tax benefits, but also in helping overcome local opposition to their actions. The search for gold has been particularly devastating to river based cultures as mercury waste toxicity destroys the water courses and Canadian corporations are active in traditional Maroon lands. On my journey I predate most of this, so I am still on the scenic route.

At the first village we stopped at, we gave out candy to the kids. I Know ... I know ... 'tisk, tisk', but the philosophy is happy children, happy mums.

After a short while we had a feeling that the mums were not that happy, and it wasn't because of dental decay.

We took Joe aside and asked him if he sensed a certain atmosphere. He went to look into it and came back to tell us that the women were upset because we were not taking photographs. Apparently tourists took pictures, and then crossed the ladies' palms with "silver". Now there was a good reason that I was not taking pictures. I was brought up to be a perfect gentleman (so I slipped up from time to time) and these ladies were wearing only short skirts.

I was not comfortable pointing my lens at a lady's breasts. None of us were, but we had to get over it and for the sake of community relations we pointed our lens at the holistic female bodies.

Typical Arawak Home

After payment, the ladies were happy, and community peace was restored.

On the subject of unhappy Bush Negro women, I have another wee story to tell. In my possession I have a pair of used Bush Negro canoe paddles. How did I obtain these ... do tell?

Excursion to Suriname

Well these are more than paddles. At that time, when a young man fell in love with a young woman, he went away, perhaps to an Alcoa mine, to make enough money to make a paddle. He needed wood, paint, and tools. When it was completed, he took it to an aunt of the girl, and the aunt presented it to the girl, and normally would encourage her to accept. After years of marriage and children, when the "bloom is off the Rose and the leaves have fallen from the vine" it is possible to buy the engagement paddles for the right price. I bought two in one village.

Continuing up river, our boat boys expertly navigated through a series of rapids, which can only be done when the river is in flood. As we approached a large bend, we could hear loud shouting and singing coming our way. Joe, our guide, suddenly seemed worried. He quickly told us that coming our way was at least one large canoe full of drunken Bush Negro men. They were going to a clan burial ground inhabited by the spirits of their ancestors. To give them courage to move amongst the spirits of the dead, they were drunk from a local alcoholic beverage.

Joe warned us not to drink anything, as it would be pushed on us, to be pleasant looking, say nothing and not to stare. Round the bend came one weaving, large canoe filled with singing and shouting males with painted faces. As good an image of bravado to be seen this side of the Andes. They eased their boat over to us with much shouting and gesticulating. I sat demurely in the boat. All the talking was in taki taki, a local dialect. I smiled and declined a drink of hooch, and apparently Joe told them that we were missionaries and didn't drink alcohol.

Excursion to Suriname

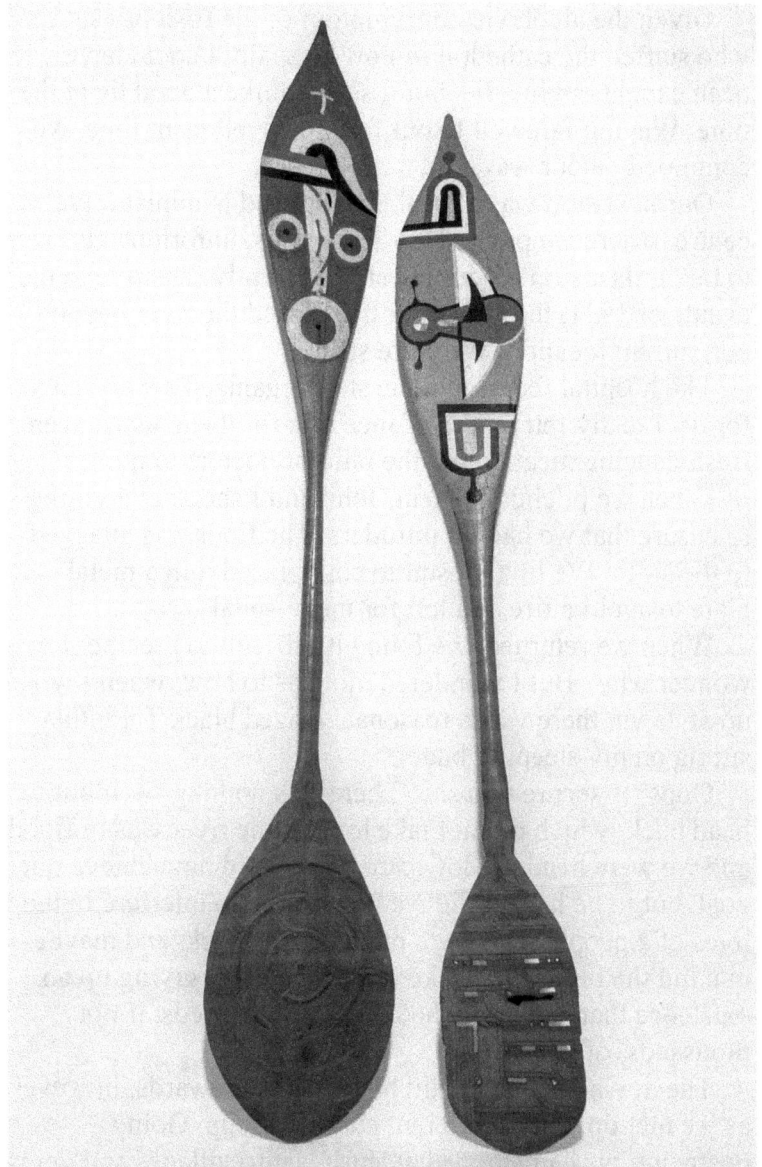

*Surinamese Bush Negro Engagement Paddles", carved by suitors for the ladies of their choice.

Excursion to Suriname

Given the alcoholic consumption of the Irish priests, who staffed the cathedral in Port of Spain, I could have been caught out in a lie, but it seemed like a good lie at the time. Waving farewell to our fellow travellers in time, we continued on our way.

Our next stop was a local hospital and administrative centre, where we pitched our tents. This, unfortunately, was to be our last stop on our quest. Apparently sensitive to the events of 1921, the Governor had closed the river beyond our current location. We were stuck.

The hospital fed us and the staff organized a wee dance for us. I really felt that the dance was for them, as we were fresh dancing meat, given the ratio of doctors to nurses.

When we pitched the tent, John and I shook everything to ensure that we had no intruders. The floor was attached to the sides. We lit a mosquito coil, placed it in a metal plate to avoid a fire and left for the hospital.

When we returned, we found it difficult to breathe. I wonder why? But I wondered more as to how, when I woke up at dawn, there was a reasonably sized black Tarantula sitting on my sleeping bag.

Oops ... secure you say. There was nothing for it but to head back, which did not take long as the river was in flood and we were heading downstream. We did not achieve our goal, but to be honest did we really need to interfere in the lives of a people who were probably in shock, and maybe making the biggest mistake of their lives by giving up an existence that had nourished them for hundreds, if not thousands, of years?

The downstream trip did have its own rewards, however, as we met up with a different cultural group. Going upstream, we had stopped at Bush Negro villages and going downstream we stopped off at a number of Arawak Amerindian communities.

Excursion to Suriname

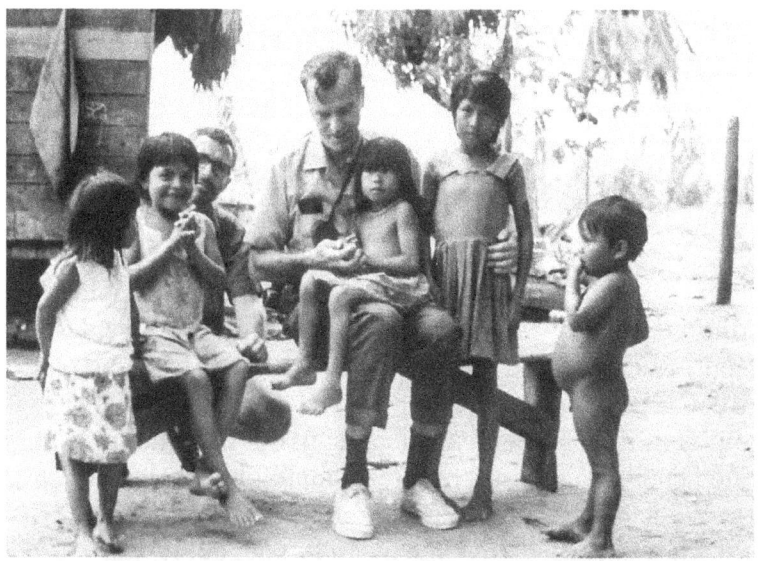

Travelling companions with Arawak Children in a village situated on the banks of Marowijne River.

The Arawaks had once been widespread from Cuba down through the islands to South America. Unlike the Caribs, who were quite warlike, the Arawaks were peaceful farmers, who grew corn, cassava, plantain, bananas, and tobacco, and hunted and fished. As with all indigenous people they were harshly treated by the Europeans and were almost wiped out. There are some island survivors, but the majority today live in Venezuela, Guyana, Suriname and French Guiana.

As with the Bush Negro villages, we saw no men, just women, children, and elderly. Their homes were more open with no side walls, just V shaped roofs which extended almost to the ground. They slept on raised platforms.

While the Bush Negroes worked largely with wood the Arawaks worked with clay and beads. Their necklaces were lovely and reminiscent of bead-work produced by the

Plains Indians of the USA and Canada, located thousands of miles away.

I purchased some necklaces, but mine I have not worn in years, as I am somewhat embarrassed. It consisted of jaguar teeth, spider monkey teeth, and nutshells. There are not many jaguars left in this world.

A brief stop in Paramaribo for shopping, and back to Port of Spain, Trinidad. I found a lovely 24-carat gold filigree pendant and chain for Eileen, of Portuguese design, and it accompanied me to Trinidad in my dirty socks. The Bush Negro paddles, I could not hide, and had to declare, but with Eileen's regrettable passing our daughter now has the pendant, and it has become a family heirloom.

We had not achieved our original goal on this trip, which was probably for the overall good, but it was unusual and original in a region that was about to change through "development" and civil war. We are still on our scenic route.

Map of South America

...

Chapter XII

Trinidad Shenanigans

One of our most enjoyable moments in Trinidad involves the Canadian Navy, and its then flagship, HMCS Bonaventure. I believe I mentioned earlier that we went to the beach every Sunday. We usually went with our Trinny friends Herbert and Nola.

This particular Sunday we arrived at Maracas Beach and parked the car beside the beach in the shade. Herbert went for a walk down the beach, where there was a bar, and the ladies set up the picnic spot.

If I am honest, I would have to say that we were also looking at bathing costumes. As we walked back, I exclaimed to Herbert that there were white men talking to our wives.

It turned out that the HMCS Bonaventure, the Canadian aircraft carrier, was anchored in Port of Spain and the crew were at the beach. They had dropped off 600 men from the army in Jamaica for joint exercises, and then taken the retiring Surgeon General (SG) of the Canadian Armed Forces on a "sail' south through the Caribbean for his retirement. Very nice if you can get it, a cruise in one of the world's biggest yachts.

We spent a pleasant time with the sailors, and at one time they started giving us a hard time about our posting in the tropics. Eileen then said that there was a downside, and that she would give a lot for a good steak or roast, given that our store's beef was all frozen, and came from halfway round the world ... Australia.

At that point one of the sailors said, "How many would you like?" He was apparently in charge of the ship's stores.

Then, quick and active minds started plotting as to how we could improve our culinary supplies. Trinidad's

Trinidad Shenanigans

Governor General was in England on a holiday, so his Bentley was available. I thought that it would be a great idea to bring some students down to the ship for a tour. They would never have an opportunity to be on a vessel like this.

It was arranged that I would come to the ship at 10:00 am the next day, and our Petty Officer friend would take me to the Bridge to meet the Officer in Charge. Herbert would arrange for the Bentley to come to the ship at 11:00 am, and Eileen and I invited the four Petty Officers for a West Indian meal at our house in the evening.

It worked like clockwork. I received permission to bring the students several days later, and then retired to the Petty Officers' mess for some very early rum. At 11:00 the GG's driver arrived with the Bentley. He was escorted to a mess and plied with rum by white men, something that had never happened to him before, and I went down to the store, where we loaded up with some grub: steaks, roasts, salmon, bacon ... which was taken to the car.

Do I feel guilty? No. Why not? Well, the meat was a drop in the ocean, and the ship had sailed to the Eastern Caribbean to give a retiring general a cruise—at an enormous cost, plus the flight deck had just been resurfaced at the cost of $100,000, and the aircraft carrier had no planes. The whole thing just seemed hilarious.

The funny thing was that the GG's driver was a police driver, and he never forgot the good time he had on the ship, plus the couple of steaks he received. I would be driving around POS when a police car or a Bentley or a prison vehicle would appear beside me, or be travelling in the opposite direction, and I would hear the vehicle's horn playing a tune for my benefit.

Trinidad Shenanigans

I am also amused to think of our food parcel in the back of a Bentey receiving a full military salute as it left the naval dockyard.

After dinner the next evening, the sailors invited us back to the ship where there was entertainment by a calypsonian, *The Mighty Sparrow*, and the Despers steel band. The flight deck had been roped off into two areas, or three if you include the musicians. In one area were honoured guests, diplomats, special citizens (including my neighbour, the only heart surgeon), officers, and some of my acquaintances. The rest was for the crew and non-honoured guests, such as us.

Sparrow, as always, was sensational. The pan was sweet and one of our new friends asked Eileen to dance, as no one was dancing. Off they went, and were immediately followed by others. It is a crime not to dance to this music.

What we did not know, because we were enjoying a great, Judith-cooked meal at our house, was that during the late afternoon an announcement had been made that since the flight deck had been refurbished, there would be no dancing.

As our Petty Officer danced with Eileen, they ended up beside the SG dancing with our neighbour's wife. When the two women started to chat, the PO said to the SG, *I see we move in the same circles, Sir*.

Unfortunately our stay in Trinidad was to end somewhat abruptly, and the origin of the problem received a kick-start in Montreal, Canada. A Professor at, what was then Sir George Williams University, was accused of racism and discrimination by a student of Caribbean descent. Anger spread like a ripple effect from the Bahamas down through the chains of island, until it reached Trinidad, where the social climate was ripe for some kind of reaction.

Trinidad Shenanigans

It all started with a demonstration by young people against the Government of Canada in downtown Port of Spain. The crowd wanted to demonstrate at the Canadian High Commission, but it was located on the upper floors of a low rise. That was somewhat problematic. Apparently the marchers couldn't find it.

The fuel for the fire of discontent was provided by chronic unemployment, latent racism, and lack of opportunities for the underclass of the black population. This is well illustrated in Edgar Mitelhouser's 1950s book, *A Morning in the Office.*

We were living in POS in 1968, and his observations seemed as relevant then. When I arrived in POS and opened an account in the local branch of a Canadian company, the manager invited me to dinner. When was the last time your bank manager invited you to dinner? I was a white person in a position of privilege.

A US naval ship anchored in POS, and a young Lieutenant, went to the Country Club to play tennis. It was a customary invitation made to officers. He was refused entry. Why? He was black. An inquiry conducted by the black Attorney General exonerated the Country Club, yet I know for a fact, that the Club was racist.

Sad to say, Trinidad was a society recovering from Colonialism/Imperialism, and opportunities often could be determined with a light meter.

The crowds seemed to become more agitated, and I took to carrying a machete under the driver's seat. One day as I stopped at a stop sign near work, two men sitting in the ditch called out "F**k you white man." I put my window down and called out "F**k you black men" and drove off.

Trinidad was losing some of its friendliness. The disturbances were a constant topic of conversation and probably more so in our house because I had constant visits

Trinidad Shenanigans

from my police friends. Little did we realize that our three-and-a-half year-old was taking it all in.

At Easter we borrowed a friend's house at Bacolet Point in Tobago. When I went to pick up a rental car at the airport, the company owner told me that he would drive us to the house because a large crowd had come over on the boat from POS, and were on a march. We just arrived at the house, located on a hilltop, when we heard loud chanting on the road below about two-km away.

Our daughter, Kelly, began to scream. It took a while to calm her down, and calm was restored only when the crowd vanished. Kelly had been listening to our conversations in the house. I decided that, since there was no obvious conclusion to the current events and with my daughter in obvious distress, to end my contract in July.

In early April, a demonstrator had been killed by police and the Black Power Movement gained momentum. Then the sugar workers went on strike, and on April 21st, the PM declared a state of emergency.

At 6:00 am the next day, I walked to the front gate to fetch the paper, when two jet fighters flew overhead. Trinidad doesn't have an air force. The markings on the plane were Venezuelan. My neighbour opposite was also walking to fetch his paper. After the usual morning greeting, he told me that the Court House was on fire, and that he was glad that his family were in New York.

TWELVE SOLDIERS HAVE MUTINIED AND RETREATED TO AN ISLAND

This was the headline in the Trinidad Express. Since everything was closed, we relaxed and went about the day. Eileen had breakfast and went to visit the heart surgeon's wife with the children. I took the dog for a walk, and Judith started her chores. At 10:00 am, the phone rang. It was a

Trinidad Shenanigans

journalist friend who told me that the US Caribbean fleet had sailed from Puerto Rico for Trinidad and Tobago. A few minutes later my friend phoned from the GG's residence. His message was somewhat fearful. He had listened to a conversation between the PM, the GG, and the captain of the Coast Guard. Half the army had mutinied, and they had the only armoured vehicles and M-15 rifles. They were also preparing to leave their Northern coastal base.

According to my friend, the Coast Guard was to sail off the coast and shell their route. Should the army reach town, there literally were hundreds if not thousands of demonstrators ready to run wild in the streets.

I immediately called Air Canada, who had no flights that day, and booked three tickets on a Pan Am flight to Barbados. Then I called our friends in Barbados and arranged for Eileen and the kids to be picked up and to stay there until things cleared up in POS.

At this point I decided to call the Canadian High Commission to see what they knew, since my information was the latest. They proceeded to give me the newspaper version, and I stopped them and told them my news. They didn't believe me, and I would not provide them with my source.

Then I went to my neighbour's, where Eileen and Mary were having a relaxing morning, and told them what was happening, and that she and the kids were going on a mini-vacation to Barbados.

My in-laws phoned from Toronto to check on us because of the international news, and told us that the Canadian Foreign Minister had assured the country that Canadians were safe, and that a Canadian destroyer was sailing to POS from Bermuda.

Trinidad Shenanigans

I have often wondered if the respected Foreign Minister knew how long it would take to make that journey.

With the family safe in Barbados and the stalemate continuing on the north coast, I and some of my neighbours amused ourselves with curfew breaking parties (excluding my Hindu alcoholic doctor). Just before 6:00 pm we would meet at a selected house where there would be food and drinks. At about 8:00 pm a police armoured car would drive up the street to check the Assistant Commissioner's house, and when they left we would stealthily retreat to our own homes.

What my friends did not know was that at about 9:30 pm the armoured vehicle would return, back up my driveway to be hidden by the trees, and the guys would come in for a few drinks with me.

The next day I received a phone call from another Canadian, Ray, telling me that I was part of his alert chain. I told him to remove me from the list because if the situation worsened, I would be the first Canadian to know, and I would not be home. I may not have friends in high places, but ultimately it is the rank and file that protect you.

We had gone to Trinidad to find out what made Trinnies tick, and our most important friends were local. I used to drink at the police sergeant's mess, my colleagues at the Country Club. My car was protected by the seeing eye of the law, and when someone did try to steal it, they were interrupted. Then the police towed it to the main barracks, where their mechanic rewired my car and I gave him a bottle of rum.

That same evening we were driven home, not in a taxi but in a paddy wagon. You can appreciate then, that it was with a certain sadness that when Eileen and I talked a few days later, we agreed that she would return to Ontario with the kids.

Trinidad Shenanigans

There can be no doubt that our sojourn in Trinidad and Tobago was a high point in our lives. It was not paradise, and there were ups, downs, and frustrations. Living next door to Deo was one. Living in a government house was another. It was difficult to get the officials to respond to a need, especially if it was wet. Trinnys had a superstition that one must not get the top of the head wet or else you got sick. Since a Trinny working class male would not be seen dead carrying an umbrella, the wet season led to a decline in outdoor productivity.

When I first moved into our house there was a 6.4 earthquake. This was interesting because I woke up with a start to complete silence. The animal/insect kingdom had gone quiet. Their sensors were much more attuned to earth tremors than ours. Then the 6.4 earthquake struck. There was little damage, except that I had a cracked kitchen sink and a cracked toilet bowl. It took months to have them replaced.

Finally in exasperation, I took a day off work and drove to the Ministry of Works to see the foreman. I was told that he was busy, so I sat down, took out a notebook and started to write, occasionally looking around me and outside at the building yard. This aroused the interest of the two guys at the front counter, and one eventually asked me what I was doing. I told them that I was a writer, and I was writing a book about Trinidad called *Trinidad and Ting,* and that the current chapter was on Cracked Toilet Bowls.

Within minutes the foreman was there, and a truck was dispatched to my home with a new bowl and sink. A plumber was also dispatched from a different location, and he was a wee bit late due to a rainstorm.

On another occasion, Eileen and I had discovered that there was a special steak dinner at the upside down Hilton

Trinidad Shenanigans

Hotel on Thursdays. The beef was from the USA—not the usual Aussie meat.

After enjoying our meal, we headed to the bar and entertainment area where an acquaintance of ours, The Mighty Robin, was playing. We ordered two rum punches and waited for the show. The waiter duly arrived with our drinks and upon taking a sip, I called him back. " Hey Man", I said, "I local." "What's with this juice? Put some rum in it."

The drinks were excellent from then on.

One constantly had to remind people that one was not a tourist. I once almost bought Eileen a lovely Sari at an Indian store on Eastern Main Road, POS. As the store owner was wrapping it up he asked me if I wanted it delivered to the ship. Ship? What ship? I said. I live in St Ann's. The Indian store owner went a little pale and handed me back my money.

"What's going on?" I asked.

He replied that he would not sell it to me as the colours would run when it was washed. I never did buy a Sari in Trinidad.

The people of Trinidad, the tropical weather and beaches, carnival, steel bands, calypso, soursop ice cream, fresh mangoes and avocados from our trees, a more relaxed atmosphere, never having to wear heavy clothes, our new friends, the side trips to Venezuela and Suriname ... All and more ... truly memorable lifetime experiences on our scenic road, which are as clear in my mind today as when they happened over 50 years ago.

Chapter XIII

Back to Normality

What is normal but life itself. I fully realize now that my partner, Eileen, has passed or gone on a different journey, that it is the so-called mundane things in life that are important. These were shared experiences, maybe not as glamorous as the trips to Paris, but shared, nonetheless, with love, humour, patience, and understanding. They made the world go round.

The next 12 years were like that, and involved raising a family, owning a home, parental responsibilities, Eileen's university years, my M.Ed program in Developmental issues, household chores (e.g. Eileen cooked, and I cleaned), and so on.

The landscape rarely changed on this part of our global tour. Yet beneath the facade of normalcy, I was experiencing some discontent. I had changed in Trinidad. I realized that some of the economic and social geography that I had been taught was tainted by the colonial era in which the activities had occurred. I realized that my senior students had little knowledge of how the world works, and as I write this, I wonder if some 50 years later much has changed.

Just look at the public election results in 2024. A global green-washing of environmental issues, climate change, human rights, human inhumanity to humans, and our desecration of the natural Earth, of which we are a part.

In my attempt to address the inconsistencies and ignorance, I wrote a new curriculum for Grade XIII, called "World Problems in Development".

I convinced the Principal that it would be unique and a good idea. The History Head tried unsuccessfully to kill it.

Back to Normality

I did a survey of grade-12 students and discovered that about 100 students were interested. I convinced the Superintendent of Curriculum that it was needed. The Ministry of Education, under conservative Thomas Wells, had a policy that if there was a need and interested students, and if there were resources and qualified teachers, then permission would be granted.

Where have all the good old conservatives gone? They are no more ... gone but not forgotten ... replaced by bean counters who use the beans to fund their robber baron class interests. What I would give for a return of Bill Davis and Tom Wells, who placed a human face on politics.

But enough of this ...

In discussion with students.

We started in 1973 with three classes of grade XIII, of whom 75% were girls—an interesting observation in itself. The next year we had four classes. The History Head was almost apoplectic.

Back to Normality

I introduced African and Caribbean literature to Geography students, and when an English teacher suggested to the English head that he could teach a course on those subjects, the Head replied,

"Do you see any students from those areas in this school?"

I used a lot of films on global issues, and even had documentary filmmakers talk about their films. I involved the students in a CBC documentary on Canadian Youth and Human Rights issues. Students went to UN conferences. A multitude of guests crossed our threshold. Every year a group would go to the UN in New York for interactive sessions on Apartheid, The CIA, and the Contras, The Global trade in oil or arms.

We met with both the Israelis and the PLO (not at the same time. The Israelis would not come into the building if the PLO were there.) We also had sessions on the environment, international aid, and always met with the Canadian Delegation. Over 500 students attended these sessions.

I recently met a woman of about 60 at a concert, and in the course of a conversation we discovered that we had met many years ago on one of my trips to New York. I used to mix several groups from different socioeconomic backgrounds. She had fond memories of the trip and retained a lot of knowledge of Apartheid. Those moments are truly rewarding, and I have had quite a few.

Sadly in the current educational climate, conducted by the neocons, such activities would be impossible.

The funniest moment occurred at a wine and cheese party thrown by the parents for the staff. In the course of the event, I got talking to a Jewish lady whose children I did not teach. She asked me what I taught, and I told her. I also told her that we had just returned from New York, where we had looked at the Middle East, the oil Industry, and had met with the Israelis and the PLO.

She then asked me how the Israelis had done? I told her they had not done well—that the PLO had been young, relaxed, and answered all questions including those on terrorism. The Israelis then came in, second as per their choice, and the first thing they did was attack the humanity of the Palestinians—a big mistake, as the students knew that Palestinians were human and had similar needs to their own. The woman then asked me if I could get the Israelis to change their act. I then wanted to know if she was offering me a contract. Her response was wonderful. She said that her son should take my class. "Why?" I exclaimed.

She replied that it would piss the hell out of her husband.

What more can I say? A somewhat stationary part of the journey, but lots happening.

Chapter XIV

Our Year in Languedoc

It was quite a road trip—the four of us packed into a very large Puegot station wagon with clothing for all seasons, correspondence courses for two grade levels and Eileen's guitar. Today one can drive from Paris to the Mediterranean in six to eight hours, but in 1982, we took two days down RN-5 through the centre of France.

Our first stop was for lunch in Pouilly, where to celebrate we splurged on a bottle of Pouilly's finest white wine, which we all enjoyed in anticipation of more to come. A word to the wise, you should never let your children become accustomed to the culinary great tastes in life. You do so at your bankbook's peril. Pouilly Fuisse is a very nice wine, but not cheap. We also regrettably introduced the kids to lobster ... Yikes! $$$$.

We were on the road again, and it doesn't get much better than this ... *les fermes, les châteaux*. It was August and the countryside was at its best, singing to us as we drove by. We also realized that as the kids were 16 and 14-years old, this adventure was the last time we would spend quality time together for this length of time (almost a year).

There is a certain feeling of liberation in knowing that no one knows where you are; your responsibilities are solely to yourselves.

Eventually we started to climb onto the Massif Central and onto the startling Karst topography of the *Causse de Larzac*. Here we encountered many sheep for the first time, and the air was filled with the smell of thyme and other spices so essential to the production of magnificent cheeses such as Rochefort. We were getting close to our home base for the next year.

Our Year in Languedoc

The descent towards Lodeve was very steep, and strained our driving skills with the heavily laden car. Little did we know that these skills would be further challenged trying to negotiate the narrow streets of the medieval village of Soubes, our temporary home.

The house was built to include remnants of the 12th century wall, and had arrow slots as windows on the lowest floor. The walls were thick stone, designed to keep out intruders and also the heat, making the lower levels quite cold in winter. This was a surprise as we had not imagined that being so close to the Mediterranean Sea we would feel cold. At that time I had taken to sleeping *au naturel* and the first time I "jumped" onto the bedsheets, I literally bounced back off the bed, thoroughly chilled.

Object lesson: Pyjamas are essential in an old stone house.

Liberty ... Fraternity ... and ... Bureaucracy

We arrived in France 11 years before the creation of the European Union. Why is this important? We are dual citizens of Canada and Ireland. This means that we have both Canadian and European passports, and don't need a visa to live in France. In 1982, we obtained student visas to attend the University of Paul Valery in Montpellier, Languedoc, and to live in Soubes, about 35-miles from the university. Once in Soubes, we needed to register with the Maire and obtain a resident's permit (*carte de sejour*)

The secretary of the mayor's office did not want to be bothered with the paperwork and asked us if we planned to visit Spain within the next three months. Since Spain was less than two hours away on the highway, we said yes. If we left France inside a three-month period we didn't need the permit. Great ...

Our Year in Languedoc

Carcassonne

Our Year in Languedoc

Then we went to the university to find out that we couldn't register at the university without a *carte de sejour*. They said that they would apply on our behalf, so we filled out the necessary forms and went in search of a photo booth to obtain three passport photographs each. Under 18's need not have a *carte*.

As part of the process, the French State needed to know that we were financially sound. I was on a Sabbatical at 80%salary, and had a letter stating that fact. However, I had to write my own letter stating that fact and sign it.

Eileen needed similar proof that as my spouse she was covered, so I asked them for more paper and I would write the letter. Oh ... no ... no. That would not do. The two letters had to be identical. I needed a photocopy of my own letter, and so we went to the designated photocopy shop, only it was closed for lunch. Two hours later we returned successfully to the Registrar's office, only to find out 20 minutes later that we needed four more passport pictures each in order to register at the university ... Bureaucracy thy name is ...

Our car was a Renault Quatre L, at that time one of over 12-million made and cheap, great on gas and made of thin metal. This was a benefit because dents were common, and they were easy to push out, and the car was very light, and it could be pushed out of tight spots—often the case with university parking. It had a bayonet gear lever through the dash, and was fun to drive, easy to park, not great on the narrow right angle turns that one finds in medieval pre auto streets, but a workhorse.

The car was off-white and there were literally thousands of off-white Quatre L's in the region and hundreds in the university parking lot. How to find one's car became an issue, until Kelly suggested a solution: Paint a caricature on the hood, and the car's name on the

Our Year in Languedoc

back. All of our cars have personal names. She was quite a good artist, and at one time developed a cartoon character, Hermie. She drew a large lady dressed in a French blue dress with red shoes and a red beret on the front of the car and her name, Tilley, on the back. We were quite the talk of the village and had a daily audience for the painting.

Five days a week, Eileen and I would head off to Montpellier and a school bus picked up the village kids including ours. We picked them up afterwards in Lodeve, and usually had time to sit at an outdoor café for a few beers and Fanta Limon. Could life get any better or worse?

Life in the village was somewhat reserved. There was a bar owned by the President of the nearby town, Lodeve, rugby club, who had a real shine for the Irish. He signed me up as a member of the local club and I received a membership card, for which I had to supply the necessary passport photo. This passport photo is big business in France.

I never saw the team play, nor visited the clubhouse, if there was one. When I tackled him once about this, he told me that they weren't very good, and he would be embarrassed for me, a former player in Ireland, to watch them. So much for my enjoyment of French rugby. The bar/café had a jukebox, and so the local teenagers hung out and played the same tunes over and over again. We made great use of the outdoor patio.

The village had a walking group that met once a month, and we joined them. We walked along old Roman roads past prehistoric dolmens, ruined fortifications and striking scenery. The group would stop for a picnic lunch, always with homemade wine which they shared with us. It was divine.

Our Year in Languedoc

On the subject of wine, we had observed people buying six-litre plastic jugs of wine in the *supermarché*. The price was right—seven francs, but what of the flavour? Finally, we splurged, and we can attest it made a very good toilet bowl cleaner.

The village also held community dinners every six weeks, and as residents we were invited and ate heartily of soups and chicken, accompanied by chunks of fresh bread, and hunks of Rochford Cheese The cheese alone was probably worth about $60.00 in Ontario, and was cut from a huge wheel.

Someone painted *Les Anglais Dehors* on the post office, but not being English, we ignored it.

Village life was relaxing. There was a small shop with a limited supply of vegetables and groceries, and a bakers van dropped off fresh baguettes. A butcher had a small shop cut into the *château* wall. His ham was wonderful, but he was fascinated by the Canadian Arctic and would ask the same questions over and over again.

Our house had no garden. No houses did, as most people had small holdings outside. We had a large patio, which overlooked the priest's vegetable garden. He had obviously never heard of St. Francis of Assisi, as he had a string of dead birds hanging across his garden to create a scarecrow effect.

One day as we looked over the wall, he took out his willy and proceeded to water his tomato plants. Since we had seen him selling vegetables to the local store, we restricted our purchases to baguettes and canned goods.

In the spring the verdant river valley was rich with wild asparagus and wild leeks. The downside of this bounty from nature is that one had to be an early riser and move quickly to taste the wild juices, as the local women were fine-tuned to the riches of the natural world.

Our Year in Languedoc

The local school did not live up to our expectations. Teaching was largely a one way transmission system, and with a substantial North African population in Lodeve, there was some racial tension. Kelly and Patrick had no experience of this, given our Trinny friends, and were uncomfortable. Kelly should have been attending the Lycee, but we wanted them to attend the same school, therefore her classmates were younger.

Patrick's English teacher made him sit in a corner with his back to the class during a test, in case he helped his classmates cheat. I was enraged, and told both kids that if a teacher ever did anything like that again, they were to walk out, find the other, and walk home, about a three-km trek. Then another one of his teachers wrote on a paper, *if I said that this was good French, I would be lying*. That was it, we pulled them out at the end of the semester, and they completed their Ontario correspondence courses with honours. Because they completed the semester in France plus the correspondence courses, they ended up with four extra credits each.

Our university courses were not much better, with a lot of talking heads and an emphasis on grammar and red ink. Eileen's French professor went to Paris for a week for a conference on the Subjunctive, and to establish some clarification on the subject. Apparently after a week the only result was that they agreed that there was a Subjunctive.

Our professor, teaching The Culture of France, clearly told us that the south of France had been under the influence of Greece and Rome, while the north had been settled by barbaric Goths, Visogoths and Celts. As a result, the north were barbarians and the south were civilized.

Our Year in Languedoc

Later, while touring France, I told a Librarian in Vannes, Brittany, that story, and boy, was she enraged.

We dropped out at the end of the first semester also. Eileen stayed home with the kids, and we hired a teaching assistant to come over and engage them all in conversational French. I switched to a small organization that specializes in helping foreign graduate students master French well enough to enrol in PhD programs. This really worked for me. The course was organized in five-day units with a pretest, an interactive course, and then a post test. I thrived except for one thing. On Monday and Tuesday, I was fine. On Wednesday, I needed two Tylenol at the end of classes. On Thursday, I had three Tylenol and on Friday, I took one before I left the house, and three at the end of the day. I specialized in Tylenol French, but it worked, and I have a Diploma that says so.

I feel blessed that we spent that year together in France and visited Spain, Netherlands, the Rhinelands and Switzerland. We did this before the crowds of modern tourists. Spain with the peseta was a better proposition than Spain with Euros, at least when you are converting from the Canadian dollar.

We covered a lot of territory in Tilley the Toiler and I would have loved to bring her back to Ontario. I have often said that if the euro, and the can dollar were at par, I could have retired to the south of France.

We exchanged houses with a couple north of Nice, rented a boat and cruised on the Canal du Midi, and revisited France whenever possible. Paris is our favourite city, and I have never seen NO DOGS OR IRISH signs that I have seen in London.

I used to fly Air France a lot, but now I have switched to Iceland-air as I have discovered Iceland, but not for a long stay. The following will always be a family memory:

Our Year in Languedoc

Carcassonne, Les Châteaux, scenic routes on coastal Med, Giverny, Nimes, Avignon, Nice, Cannes, Cape D'Agde, Mont St Michel, the markets and many more.

There were many scenic routes on this trip, and I would be remiss if I did not mention the ten-week circumnavigation of Western Europe and the side trips to Morocco and Pisa, Florence and Venice.

Chapter XV

Education for a Global Perspective (EGP)

How to bring world issues into the classroom, and the school and to incorporate the classroom, and thereby the students, into the world.

I have always felt that a global perspective is like a lens in a pair of glasses. Once you place the lens on your eyes you will see the world and your place in a very different way, change your behaviour and act accordingly. Like any normal pair of lenses, the preparation for EGP requires careful preparatory work, such as the development of a clear definition, a conceptual framework, curriculum, and creative resources.

This is not the time nor is there the space for a treatise on EGP, but it behooves me to say something on the topic, as it played a crucial role in paving my scenic journey.

Before I started my position as Coordinator of EGP, a joint project of The Ontario Teachers' Federation and The Canadian International Development Agency, I was told that I had to know everything there was to know about EGP, and I initiated a library search of the topic and read everything the library found.

Of course, in order to get the job I had clearly demonstrated that I was familiar with the content areas of International Development, Human Rights, Environmental Issues, and Peace Education, and had worked with and sat on the Boards of Non-Governmental Organizations active in these fields In my M. Ed, I had concentrated on the educational needs of developing nations.

Nothing like this had ever been tried before on this scale, and it is with immense pride that I accepted the role as creator of a project that could ,in a perfect world, lead in many positive directions. I didn't achieve the ultimate

Education From a Global Perspective (EGP)

success of changing the face of education as we know it, but we did make quite a marked short term impact.

The project had over 12,000 teachers on our contact list. We produced a quarterly newsletter that went to the 12,000 and every school in the province. A number of the large school boards had EGP committees and their own programming.

We worked with every school District in the province, including the Far North, except one where the Director reportedly said that the issues listed earlier were communist. This man was obviously an early MAGA republican.

EGP concepts were throughout the common curriculum of the early 90s. I worked with OISE staff on the creation of the Transformative Learning Centre and taught a course for them. The Faculty of Education at the University of Toronto created a Global Education department and attracted two English profs from the University of York to staff it. EGP is a part of the official policy of the Ontario Teachers' Federation.

My partner and I trained 16 *Train the Trainers* to deliver five-day training conferences for teachers through the province for all Boards, but on teams of four teachers. The trainers consisted of three English-speaking groups and one Francophone, and between them, they delivered 20 five-day institutes in isolated resorts throughout the province. I had the funds to hire replacement supply teachers for all events, and a key strategy was to invite each Board to send a Superintendent for Lunch on the Monday. This was at a time when generally teachers did not smile at Supers, but not at these sessions. The participants were beaming, thus causing the Supers to at least smile ... a winning moment, as a favourable report would undoubtedly be made.

Education From a Global Perspective (EGP)

We had created a winning program, and to match it in curriculum development, we had eight pilot projects: writing curriculum in English, French literature, Grade X Science, Home Economics, an EGP elementary school, an EGP secondary school, a role for NGOs in school programming, and integrating a school Peace Garden in school programming.

I don't know what you think as you read this, but I feel that it was amazing. I had tried to reach every group invested in public education, and I met with them all, including parents and students who were not included in my original description. The program was so successful, that I went in to my immediate superior at OTF and complained to him that he had not adequately prepared me for my job.

Pierre was visibly upset by my comment, and wanted to know what I was talking about. I told him that I don't know how to reply to "Fan Mail". I was receiving letters and emails saying such things as,

" Where have you been all my teaching life?"

Thankfully, as a result of my grammar school education and my parents' guidance, modesty became me.

Unfortunately, despite an excellent outsider's evaluation report we had a big, big flaw. We were not independent financially. We depended on the in kind contribution of OTF and a cash infusion from the Federal Government. In a fit of anger about criticisms of the Liberals foreign policy by groups identified as Global Education Centres (nothing to do with our program), the government cut our funding and may have used an expletive in the process. I had a close friend in the room who filled me in on all the details. In fact his parliamentary assistant, an MP formerly linked to an NGO, connected us to the offending groups.

Education From a Global Perspective (EGP)

"*C'est la vie*". A write-in campaign with thousands of letters to Chretain failed to achieve anything. It is interesting that these programs were created when a Conservative government was in power and were killed by the Liberals.

The OTF could have kept the program going in a reduced form as they had the money, but in my view they were more interested in politics and their own individual organizations than an OTF project.

Ultimately because the Conservatives won the next provincial election, and M. Harris, "Trump light" and his former truck driver, J.Snobelen, new Minister of Education, seemed determined to remove anything progressive from education, and also take about $ Two-billion from education. The mechanistic bean counters were in control and much of what we had accomplished disappeared, except for small pockets of resistance. EGP had disappeared into the mists of time, but my scenic route remained open.

Because of my work, I made some global contacts and continued the scenic route. I delivered papers at conferences in Los Angeles, Toronto, Univ of Western Ontario, Queen's Univ, St. Mary's Univ, Nairobi, Randers Denmark, Indianapolis, Peace Univ, (Costa Rica).

I worked with some NGO's in The Philippines, and went fishing in a dugout canoe on a moonlit night on the South China Sea. After four-hours of fishing, we only caught four fish. Overfishing by large boats from Manilla was destroying the inshore fishery ... a worldwide problem.

While I had been out fishing in an outrigger canoe, with my bottom a mere six-inches above the South China Sea, and the scene illuminated by the brightest and largest heavenly moon you have ever seen, an army patrol had visited the village. The fisher-folk were happy that I was not there, as they did not want to have to explain to the army as to who I was and why I was there. After all, my work involved empowering the fisher-folk to be independent of major business interests. I had the distinct impression that the fisher-folk feared the army and rebels equally.

When in Kenya, we visited our Maasai friends and spent a month with them, travelling around and staying at the mansion of the Paramount Chief. Here there was no running water, as elephants had trampled the pipes.

Me with two Maasai

We were really privileged to be allowed, as non Maasai, to sit in on a council meeting.

We stayed in the Maasai Mara Lodge as the guests of the Chief Game Warden, our friend's cousin. I forgot to mention that our friend was the second child of the fourth wife of the Paramount Chief. We did not know this before we arrived, as she had never mentioned this in Toronto.

Education From a Global Perspective (EGP)

Thanks to our friends we saw every possible animal except for a leopard, and we had a bonus as her father was protecting a pair of White Rhinos, which we were able to stroke. They were protected by special fencing and heavily armed guards.

Another highlight occurred when we spent an evening at a Dutch sponsored agricultural project, the Ilkerin Loita Integral Development Project. The discussions were so deep and interesting, especially on the potential role of women, that when the diesel powered lighting went off at 10:00 pm, the Maasai farm manager, Mark, turned them back on until the small hours of the morning.

Eileen and I were known as Mzungus with a difference, i.e., a different type of foreigner. They had never expected white people to relate to them the way we did. Probably just as well I didn't enter the British Colonial Service. I would at that time have been a different Mzungu.

In our honour the Maasai had killed a goat for the evening meal. We had been avoiding meat, but felt that we might insult their political leadership. The goat lasted about 30 mins inside me, and then it desperately needed to leave. This became somewhat awkward as they had modern toilets, but several days ago a herd of charging elephants had trampled the water lines to shreds ... no plumbing.

When we stayed at the Maasai Mara Park as a guest of the chief Game Warden, we watched a stampeding herd of elephants, and they were quite impressive. We saw every one of the major animals with the exception of a leopard, which hunts at night. One had invaded the Chief's compound and stolen a goat without drawing any attention to itself.

Education From a Global Perspective (EGP)

Traditional and Modern Maasai homes

The cheetah is a different story. Apparently they don't relate well to the tourist trade, and have turned from a daytime hunter relying on their speed to a night hunter, where speed is not too helpful. As a result their numbers were in decline.

We witnessed the tourist phenomenon first hand. We were tourists after all. Saroni stopped the 4-Runner near a Baobab Tree where a pride of lions had recently finished lunch, and within 30 minutes there were eight tourist jeeps encircling the pride. The drivers all have radios and spread the news.

There are many stories associated with EGP, some short, some long. One of the funniest occurred at a resort near Gananoque, Ont. One of our guest teachers was Bill Commander, a master Algonquin canoe maker, who has four canoes in the Canadian Canoe Museum. Bill wanted to perform a sunrise ceremony, and we all assembled on the lawn at sunrise. As he was about to light the fire, the Manager came racing out pushing a wheelbarrow. His fire

Education From a Global Perspective (EGP)

Rare White Rhinos

Education From a Global Perspective (EGP)

insurance would not allow an open fire on the premises. How many sunrise ceremonies have been performed using a wheelbarrow? ... I wonder.

I have many memories and I would like to share one with the readers. At an event, I made a commitment to visit a small elementary school in Belleville Ontario. Unfortunately, in the scheduled week I lost my voice, always an annoyance for a trained public speaker. With sincere apologies we rescheduled for February 1991.

That day turned out to be day-two of the outrageous US invasion of Iraq. Colin Powell Lied to Congress and the UN, Tony Blair lied to the UK parliament, Hassan was no saint, but remember, he, early in his career, was a paid assassin for the CIA—paid to eliminate Iraqis of a communist persuasion.

The reality was that Canadians, on the morning news, were watching the bombardment of Iraq by land, air and sea. I know of kids in the Beaches area of Toronto, who imagined that the ships were in Lake Ontario and that their lives were threatened. I was very distressed, and had no idea what I was going to say to the children. I was so angry about Tony Blair's deceit that I sent my UK passport back, and became an Irish citizen as well as Canadian. The Grammar school's little Englishman lasted about 40-years.

As we approached Belleville—a blank slate. My mind refused to function, but as they say, necessity is the mother of invention. There I was on stage in the cafetorium. The children entered, with the youngest at the front, all sitting on the floor ... What to do???????. There were about three to 400 children ... Pressure ... and then it hit me.

I introduced myself, and then I asked each child to relax and breath deeply; it is important to breathe. They

Education From a Global Perspective (EGP)

had to close their eyes and keep them closed ... no peeping. I told them that I was going to make a number of statements and if they liked one, they should put up a hand and keep it up.

It is summer and I am lying on the beach soaking up the sun. Hands went up.

When I grow up I want to be a hockey player and play in the NHL Hands went up.

When I grow up I want to be a nurse or a doctor and help the sick. Hands went up.

When I grow up I want to be a teacher. Some hands went up, and some came down.

When I grow up I want to follow in the family business or farm. Some hands went up.

When I grow up I want to see a world in which there are no wars. I want to see a world at peace.

The rest of the hands went up.

I then asked the group to open their eyes and look around the room. I was almost knocked off my feet by the surge of energy emanating from the group. It was infectious. The children were all smiling. They had found a common ground to which they all belonged. I had an inflatable Earth Ball, which I then batted into the room. The students enthusiastically batted the Earth around until it came up on stage, and I grabbed it and held it tight. I then asked them what they were doing, and eventually it came to pass that the student group was abusing the planet on which we live. I then asked them how we could correct this abuse.

How far have we retreated from that evolutionary thought process? It would seem that the business and political "leadership" globally are driving us towards self-destruction and the rest of us are like sheep. This p***es me off, as not only are a few disrupting my journey, but my children's, grandchildren's, great-grandchild's, and the journeys of billions of others. What can be done????? What is the answer????? Unfortunately organized religion may not be the answer.

What if there are no "pearly gates? What if the kingdom of God is within us, and we are responsible for all our actions. The political systems are so corrupted by donors that they have become inept. Yet the children have told us what they want, Can we deliver it? Will my journey continue to be scenic?

Chapter XVI

Costa Rica

One door closes, another opens. Sometimes it feels a bit like "Sliding Doors" the movie with Glynith Paltrow, when she enters through the subway doors different scenarios occur. We bought our farm from the Union of Hotel Workers of Costa Rica, who used it as a recreational centre. However, they soon realized that hotel workers work long hours and odd shifts. As a result, the place was under-utilized, and so they put it on the market.

Again I feel that we were on a scenic route, as fate intervened and provided us with a way to transfer a substantial amount of money to San Jose, CR, without paying the inordinate fees that Canada's commercial banks wanted to charge.

Because of my contacts in the international NGO community, I found an organization that regularly handled financial transactions for others in the non-profit sector. There is a good reason that the banks are so rich, and it is good to know of ways to circumvent their traditional usury. Our Costa Rican Lawyer had a fit when she heard of our plans and warned us against it.

It is no accident that the banks are so rich due to their usurious ways, and it feels good to reduce their potential profits. Eventually she called us to tell us that a scruffily dressed man had shown up at her office and handed her a large envelope with the equivalent of $52,000 Canadian inside. Deal done in favour of the good guys.

I was now officially retired from mainstream regular work and could now combine some part-time work with stays in Costa Rica. I taught a course at The Ontario Institute for Studies in Education and also two courses at

Costa Rica

Centennial College, one on Ecotourism and the other on Human Rights in the Ontario Workplace.

Eileen and me

In CR I almost had the dream job. There is in CR a Peace University endorsed but not funded by the United Nations. It was the brainchild of Dr. Robert Muller, a former Under Secretary General of the UN, and funded by CR.

There had been a brief Civil War in CR in the late 40s, and upon winning the conflict, the victorious left abolished the armed forces, a unique global event. The resulting "Peace Dividend" is invested in the people with public Health Care and Unemployment Insurance, and employees receive an annual 13th month in salary benefits. This whole commitment to peace led to the founding of the Peace University.

Eileen and I had attended some meetings at the Peace University and I had presented a paper on our work in EGP to Dr Muller and a group of Dutch and Americans. At one such meeting the Chair of the group said that she

Costa Rica

had an announcement to make. She continued by saying that they had a proposal to make to the current President of the University, Muller having retired. They wanted to create a Masters Program in Environmental Education and Global Education, and they had found a suitable candidate to head up the program—"and he is in the room with us today ... Tom would you like to come to the front and say a few words ..."

It was as if CR had had one of its earthquakes. I was at the same time shocked, amazed, thunderstruck, and delighted. This was all news to me. No one had ever said a word to me about this program.

It was not to be. The CR President of the University was not known as a progressive thinker or as a risk-taker, and the project never left the ground. I never met the man, but funny enough, years later Maurice Strong, friend of Pierre Trudeau, Canadian businessman, former Head of the Canadian International Development Agency and also the UN Environmental Agency, became the Unie President. He brought in a South African friend to start the Master's Program that might, if I had entered the right 'subway cars', have been mine. C'est la vie encore.

"Whatever will be, will be,
The future's not ours to see ..."

We ended our stay in CR by obtaining the saplings of 44 endangered tropical hardwoods, and having our peon plant them on the soccer field. Some might think that was sacrilege, but it was our small contribution to counter the green-washing of Costa Rica, where the natural forest cover is diminishing at a surprising rate, given the existing laws that are supposed to conserve it.

Costa Rica

View of the soccer field

I have witnessed an illegal forest clearing operation in the central mountains. The chain saws could be heard for miles, and the authorities had to have known what was happening.

Hopefully our mini forest has thrived. I have no idea as we sold the property 20 years ago.

Foreign property ownership can be complicated, because of the threat of squatters moving onto your property and the legal difficulties of removing them. We had to hire someone to live on the farm. Then, because he was not completely trustworthy, we had to hire a Canadian to watch him—hire a watcher to watch the guardian. Then the watcher lost interest in the property, and the peon started to raise geese on our farm without permission. He was starting to treat the place as his own.

Geese are nasty creatures with a fearless viscous streak and gigantic poops. The peon became difficult when we told him that the geese had to go, and we had to threaten to fire him ...

Costa Rica

Poas Active volcanic crater

It was time to leave scenic CR after a 13-year adventure. —Time to leave the orchids that bloomed on our trees, the lovely motmots that nested in our hedges, the cashew tree at the top of our hill, the fresh oranges and bananas that we loved (and in our absence donated to the local senior's home), the magnificent macaws that gathered every late afternoon at the Caroni Biological Reserve to fly as a flock to overnight on an offshore island, the chattering flocks of parrots flying overhead, the ceviche at our favourite local restaurant, the hot springs at the side of Mount Arenal (its nightly flares as red streaks in the sky).

All of this and more is part of Costa Rica, and we were lucky because we arrived and left before a major tourist boom changed the Pacific coastline forever.

Costa Rica

Sloth descending to poop

Chapter XVII

Egypt

It was a typically cool grey day, a November day bracing itself for the onslaught of winter, although a winter's day in Toronto, compared to my current home in Orillia, is barely bracing. Eileen and I were in the kitchen preparing the Sunday roast for the oven. This was in the days when a Sunday roast was affordable, and a regular occurrence.

Around 4:00 pm the phone rang. Eileen answered it—said "He's right here," and shrugged her shoulders to indicate that she had no idea who it was.

It was Fran ???? (surname long forgotten). I had known him when he was with an NGO and based in Toronto. He was calling me at the behest of the President of Victoria College. Apparently she was on the management committee of an educational project in Egypt, in conjunction with UNICEF Egypt, Queen's Univ, Kingston and the University of Toronto. The project was part of UNICEF's international campaign, "Education For All."

The Egyptian Program was the brainchild of the wife of the Egyptian President, who wanted to improve the educational level of Egyptian girls. Girls learn better in an interactive, more student-centred environment, not one way transmission from a talking head. A number of Teacher Conferences have been held (at a luxury resort on the Red Sea) using interactive teaching methodologies. The project had nor been fully thought through, and an important part of the education system had been left out—namely the Inspectorate.

This group was doubly important, in that a teacher's salary depended on a favourable rating from an Inspector, a member of an older, more traditional group—a group unaccustomed to movement in the classroom, unaccustomed to students communicating in the classroom —all of which led to unfavourable ratings and complaints.

Egyptian inspectors

An additional session had been added to train 160 school inspectors, and it was due to start in two weeks. Unfortunately the English Professor of Global Education, who shall remain nameless, let them down at the last minute.

Here they were, in November, trying to find a replacement—hence Fran's question to me: did I know of anyone? I had to be honest, so I told him that the only person I knew, who was available, was me. At this point Eileen passed me a sheet of paper upon which she had written in large print,

YOU ARE NOT GOING TO EGYPT WITHOUT ME.

Message received, and within the week we were comfortably seated on Air France on our way to Cairo.

Egypt

Let the skirmishes begin and there were a few. The first one was with the hotel located on the island of Gezira in the Nile river. We declined to accept the postage stamp sized room, despite their protestations that they were full. Those Canadians ... tut, tut ... hardly diplomatic, but we were not going to be pushed around. We sat with our suitcases in the small lobby creating a veritable obstruction, until after about 40 mins, would you believe—they found a suite. We were not just being awkward, as we needed some space. We were meeting two other presenters, who we had not met, and knew nothing about, and we had three days to prepare three workshops for 160 inspectors.

There was an NGO person from Pakistan, a prof from Brock with experience in authentic evaluation, and myself. The initial plan was easy. We had three-day sessions—one day each, but helping out if necessary on other days, then three-days rest in Cairo, then another repeat three days, until we had worked with all 160.

I pointed out that as we are doing different things we needed to illustrate how each session was interrelated. We could not expect our clients to make the connections.

An interesting statement was made by a UNICEF Egypt Director later that first day. We were at a meeting to outline our proposal and introduce ourselves. I mentioned my Irish background and undergraduate work and my work later in Canada. It was pointed out to me that I should stress the Irish connection and downplay Canada (even though it was a Canadian-funded program) because Egyptians admire the Irish as the first to throw off the English yoke, and are somewhat diffident to Canadians because we tend to rubber stamp what Americans want.

This, hopefully, may have recently changed. Until the current generation of US leadership there was a lot of truth in that.

Egypt

No fancy resort for us, but less guilt. We were transported to a Menofi UNESCO Training centre in the Nile Delta, a Centre that was suffering from benign neglect. There was a hole in the mosquito netting that you could fly a 737 through, and the less said about the bidet the better.

Built as a UNESCO contribution to Egyptian development, the building had been sadly neglected. The bidet in the bathroom was not functional, as the water pipe protruded some six-cm above the rim of the bowl, and was rusty to boot. We were also worried about the food, and I ended up with a few cases of the runs, which is not conducive to running an all day workshop program. Did I mention that somehow I ended up delivering the first day of each three-day set?

Eileen and I went to check the presentation room and, true to form, it was set up in typical 'talking head' format. We rearranged the seating in circles of eight, and retired. In the morning the room was back in 'talking head' format, with the addition of a head table.

Upon inquiring as to what was happening, I was informed that the Assistant Deputy Minister of Education was coming to address the troops.

The troops reference was not me being facetious, the ADM was indeed a Captain in the army, and he did apparently lay out his expectations. Luckily he did not try the same stunt with me for there might have been an Irish-inspired coup in Egypt that night. I always respond to requests, but I don't react well to orders, as the Principal of GDCI discovered years before. As it was, we were invited to share the head table with him, but luckily for me, I needed to speak with the Arabic/English translator and clue her in as to what to expect.

Egypt

The Inquisition over ... the ADM departs, and we reorganize the room. Our method to form groups is a well-used one.

We had 60 participants and would work with eight groups. We have the group stand in a circle with their eyes closed, and no talking is the rule. We tell the group that we are going to place a coloured sticky paper dot on their forehead, and that we would always tell them when we were going to do it. When everyone has a dot we would invite them to form a group based on their colour without talking. I should add that we always invite people to participate as occasionally one meets an introverted person who is very uncomfortable with the process. We would rather have that individual watch, than spread negative energy to the process.

This being an Islamic country, Eileen was to place the dots on the females, and I, the males, and I immediately had an embarrassing moment. These devout Muslims had been bowing to the ground for many years, and as a result quite a number had a circular depression in the middle of their foreheads ... right where I normally place the dot ...

What to do?????? If I place it in the centre of the depression am I insulting them? Do place it above, below, right or left? Does it matter? It must be uniform no matter what I decide.

Things fell apart with the second group, and thankfully it had nothing to do with either Eileen nor I. Although an unpaid observer, Eileen became our unofficial manager and helped everybody, participants, interpreters (two) or staff. Such was her character.

My session with the second group was fine, but I was having tummy issues and on day two I was relaxing in bed

Egypt

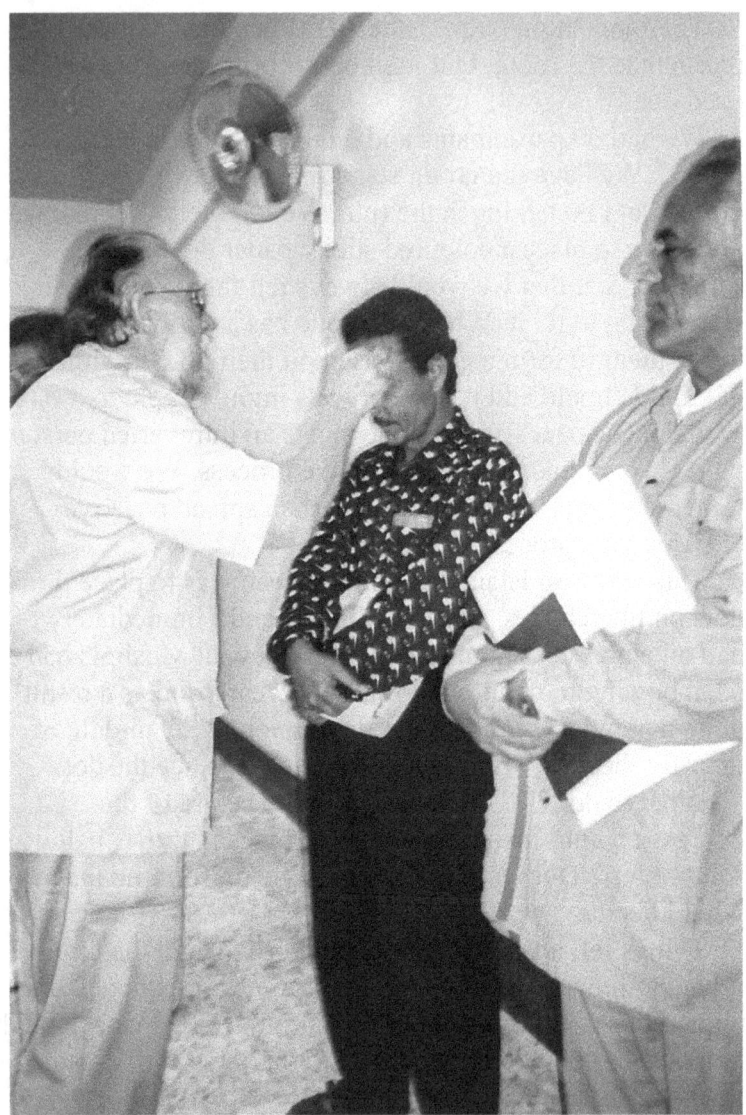

Placing coloured dots

when Eileen burst into the room and told me that I had to come quickly as there had been an incident and the Egyptians were threatening to walk out. Also the Ministry

Egypt

of Education and UNICEF had called, and a woman from the Canadian Embassy wanted to talk to me ... *Why me?* I thought? *I am neither the team leader nor Pharaoh.*

In fact there was no team leader, outside the short MOE Captain, and he only controlled the participants. Eileen said that as far as she was aware the Canadian Prof had made a comment about Egyptians, and this was loud enough to be heard and understood. Eileen had not heard it; the Prof couldn't recall it, and the Egyptians were not talking to us.

What a mess, and it all blew up so fast.

Apparently the Prof was using coloured candy to form groups, and she got upset when some of them were eaten and others were switched so that participants could sit with their friends. It was eventually reported that the Presenter said, *these Egyptians can't do anything right.*

By the time we found all of this out, the prof had packed her suitcase and was trying to find a taxi to the airport. I wouldn't let her go, as it was getting late, and convinced her to sleep on it. In the morning, cooler heads prevailed along with many Canadian mea-culpa. She apologized. I apologized, and maybe that was why the Embassy lent us a vehicle and driver to go to Saquara. I saw the possible headlines in the Toronto Star ...

Canadian Educators Cause a Diplomatic Incident in Egypt.

The best group to work with was the third and last group. Was it because we were better performers with several sessions under our belt or was it the group itself and their personalities.

Whatever the reason, we had the best reaction. One participant came up to tell me that he had studied the Quran and that he had identified certain passages in the Holy Book that mirrored some of the things I had said. This was quite a shock as I did not identify with any religious group,

Egypt

but maybe it was because my favourite church was the Cathedral of the Trees.

I gave him my card and asked him if could send me the relevant passages. I pointed out to him that I lived in a district of Toronto that had a large number of Arabic-speaking shops and that I was sure that I could have them translated. He agreed to send them, but alas they never arrived.

The same group organized an evening of entertainment, and we were invited. Some of the women were of Bedouin heritage, and they were dressed accordingly. They regaled us with their songs and unique chants.

Eventually it was our turn. What to do? How many rousing Canadian songs did we know? Eileen remembered an old girl guide campfire song that is probably best forgotten, but we sang it anyway. Who would know if we sang the wrong words or missed a verse? Eileen was of Irish extraction, and I am Irish, so there was a core group of songs that we knew. We entertained our Arabic speakers with rousing versions of Galway Bay, Danny Boy and When Irish Eyes Are Smiling. It was fun, if only more nationalities could learn to laugh and sing together.

On the last day a participant came up to me to thank me for the program. He said that he would be honoured if we would come to his village the next day for lunch, and the community would put on a show for us. I replied that we would be honoured to come. It was something that I really wanted to do, to meet people in their normal circumstances.

We had already visited the Pyramids at Giza and the National Museum with King Tut's exquisite golden stuff. You know they have so many historic coffins and mummies that they simply give each one a number e.g.: A1, A2, etc.

Egypt

To our great dismay, there was a message at the front desk in the morning from the Canadian Embassy telling us that the Ministry, or should I say The Military, had cancelled the visit, and we never saw our new friend again. *Quel dommage*. This is what happens when one lives in a military state. Another door opened in that the Embassy offered us a Toyota Land-cruiser plus driver for a trip to Saquara, where there is a multiplicity of Pharaonic sites including the famous Step Pyramid.

On the way the driver stopped at a carpet factory, where we observed either an absence or the abuse of child labour laws. Interesting but even today, many years later, my second choice.

Chapter XVIII

The Asian Component of our Journey

As a private consultant, I visited a number of Websites, looking for interesting positions and found one with a Foundation in China. I applied but missed the cut. However about a month later I saw the ad again. Throwing pride out the window, I reapplied again and bingo, I am on my way to Chengdu and Xining via Hongkong.

In my contract I was to evaluate an existing privately-funded education program for Tibetan children, and also teach the basics of interacting student learning to Chinese, Tibetan and Uighur teachers of maths, sciences and language. The evaluation was supposed to include a site visit to the Chinese part of the Tibetan Plateau. The Chinese would not issue me a visa for Tibet, so the organization had arranged for some Tibetans to come to me, and also hired an interpreter.

My first experience was of a more commercial nature. In a casual office conversation on laptops, they said that I should get more memory as memory was dirt cheap in China. Next minute my interpreter and I were taking a taxi to what on the outside appeared to be a large apartment building.

Inside the building was something quite different. Each suite was an electronic store selling every type of electron gadget you could name. It was so large it took us ages to find the Acer store. Once it was established that we wanted memory, the negotiations began. I wasn't exactly sure what was transpiring and was somewhat hesitant in my response, but I did notice that the more I hesitated, the lower the price became, so I stalled and stuttered until she didn't budge. Once we had a deal, a girl appeared from nowhere, grabbed my laptop and vanished. The salesclerk then proceeded to tell me that I had a one-year warranty and that I should be very careful in China as everything is fake.

My client and I then flew to Xining and stayed in a very modern hotel and conference centre where my first night's sleep was interrupted by a phone call from, literally, a lady off the night. The receptionist said that they knew nothing, but they lied, as all calls were routed through the front desk. Some years later, in a casual conversation with a university professor in Serbia, she mentioned that she too had a similar call, while in China, and accepted the invitation.

To this day I still do not know whether she was toying with me or not. I did not recommend her for the position she was applying for, but not because of China.

I very quickly got tired of the food as they used a lot of canola oil, probably of Canadian origin. Cathy (not her real name) came to the rescue. This amazing woman had created an Italian Restaurant entirely through Google, the menu, the paintings, and decorations, all. She also had internet on the ground floor, so I could Skype Eileen daily.

Cathy also told me that the social mores had changed for the worse. Ten years previous, if I dropped my wallet on the ground at her door, it would still be there a year later. By the year 2000, the wallet would be gone in seconds.

My first training session was interesting. The room had been set up for a Talking Head, and I changed it to my favourite series of circles. At 9:00 am the doors opened, and the first participants entered, looked around, and promptly left the room. I decided to say nothing and wait

The Asian Component of our Journey

Me holding a Red Panda

The Asian Component of our Journey

to see how long the penny took to drop, before we started our first topic: Why do we work in groups?

I also issued sticky notes and asked them if they would kindly turn off their cell phones, place their name on the sticky, and let us guard them. We got them all, but for the Ministry Officials, who were probably there to watch me in case I was some kind of deviant. The government in China is ever-present. Even every radio station still has a military detachment stationed beside it.

I think that the workshops went well despite me developing a horrible cold, which I liberally attacked with hot, black coffee and Scotch whisky.

Because they had brought people to Xining from Lhasa, my clients decided to have a three-day conference in the middle of the program. To facilitate me, they lent me a new Land-cruiser, a driver, and Sodar (my interpreter for a three-day adventure). I was responsible for food, gas, and hotels.

We headed off to Rebkong, an important Tibetan town in Western China, where there is a significant artist community close by. On the way, we passed part of the Great Wall, however I was still under the weather and I passed on the opportunity to climb to the top.

Further along the road we were pulled over by a soldier on a motorcycle. Thankfully he ignored me and said nothing. We sat there for about 20 minutes when a military convoy passed by. The centrepiece of this show of might was a truck loaded up with a gigantic rocket, which explains the superhighway we were driven along. There was little traffic and few settlements, but this road led up to the Province, which was the centre of their missile and space program.

Our driver's home village was a walled community with a very high thick clay wall surrounding not only the village, but also each family compound. This is perhaps indicative of the insecurity felt within the Tibetan community in China.

Our first call was with the driver's grandmother, where we sat on a raised platform for some traditional hospitality involving tea drinking. After the very sweet, thick Chai, we went to an artist's compound, where the painter was adding the finishing touches in gold leaf to a Buddhist prayer scroll of the Goddess TARA. It turned out that TARA had travelled widely in the dim distant past. Not only is she a Hindu and Buddhist Goddess, but she is a mountain in Croatia, and a hill in Ireland, where historically the High Kings of Ireland were crowned, and where my daughter and I have trod. Tara represents the embodiment of perfected wisdom and is the mother of all Buddhas.

Eileen liked to collect artwork from our journeys, and I was on the lookout for some Tibetan work. We left the village for Rebkong. Here we found cultural centres and art galleries, but the works for sale seemed to be a mite pricey ... tourists ... tourists. I decided to revisit Tara in the morning and after our driver picked us up, we headed back to his village.

Sodar and the driver insisted that I stay in the SUV while they negotiated on my behalf. After a suitable interval they returned with a suggested price of $70.00 US ... SOLD. The amount of gold leaf alone was probably worth that, and TARA proudly hangs on my wall with the providence /photographs of me, with the artist securely attached to the back.

On the way back to Xining we had to cross several ranges of mountains through tunnels, and at the first range there was a traffic delay. Suddenly near a garage, our driver abruptly left the vehicle and disappeared, only to

The Asian Component of our Journey

reappear in a few minutes with several pieces of thick rope. Apparently it had snowed in the mountains since our earlier passage and the police were checking cars for snow tires or chains. No one without these accessories shall pass.

Now our four-runner was only one month old, and the tires were superior, but they did not pass muster. Our ingenious driver proceeded to wrap the rope around the tires on the driver's side of the vehicle, and then he drove up to the checkpoint. The police were standing in the middle of the highway, checking the tires on the driver's side only, and so we passed with honours.

As soon as we were out of sight of the checkpoint, the driver pulled over and removed the unsightly and rough riding ropes, and we sped on our way.

Upon exiting the first tunnel we were surprised to find that the offensive snow was only a few centimetres thick, and was being swept by the latest in Chinese snow-removal equipment: women in orange jumpsuits armed with broomsticks.

Back to work in an enjoyable series of workshops. Tibetans and Ughirs like to play, and we experimented with learning and had fun. On our final day we gathered together for a ceremony, which involved drinking some very strong alcohol. I was allowed to merely sip the dangerous brew. In addition, a teacher made a speech thanking me for my work. It was quite an honour as he draped a white silk shawl over my shoulders and thanked Canada for sending me as they had previously sent Norman Bethune. Now, don't get me wrong, I don't in no way equate myself with Bethune, but I felt proud that they had found meaning in our work together.

The Asian Component of our Journey

After that evening, we had a group meal with some drinking and singing, and I taught them to sing *en français* : *Alouetta, Alouetta* ...

I later received a text from my interpreter looking for the words of *Alouette* for his university professor in China. However, as doors opened on the journey, they also closed, only to be opened again. Asia was out, but with the rest of the cash we went on a Danube cruise to celebrate our 50th wedding anniversary. It was one of the best trips we had been on, although on the trip we had an indicator that Eileen had some health issues, which were to throw some curve-balls our way over the coming years.

Still, Tara remains on my wall, and the white silk shawl adorns a living room chair.

Chapter XIX

Musings from a Boat on the Canal du midi, 2006

By Eileen and Tom

As you can see, this was written some years ago as a joint effort by the two of us, and as Eileen has departed on a different journey, it seemed important to me that since she was an integral part of this journey, some of her special writing should be included.

In our journey together, I had often goaded her to do this or do that to illustrate her brilliance as she had a much more quirkier mind than I had .... altogether a quicker thinker, but she was her own person, who did it her way, and so with great pride I include some of her musings in this work.

Saturday September 16th ... Capestang just before dawn:

We had woken up around 4:30 am in the cramped cabin of our fairly cheap 36-ft cabin cruiser, a little sore in places we didn't know existed. This had been quite the learning experience in that one should never rent the cheapest boat. It is cheaper for a reason.

Everything was still; even the canal had a glassy look to it. This would not last for long as the early birds were restless, and a purple ring peeked nervously at the horizon. All was quiet—the tricolours hanging limply from most boats ... crew still asleep. The Dutch barge—the perky pointy prow pointing skywards—an attitude that reflects its ability to transcend both sea and canal.

The broad-beamed boats of the Connoisseur take up more than their fair share of the canal. These are serious, sophisticated sailors on a World Heritage site that closes

Musings from a Boat on the Canal du Midi, 2006

down at 7:00 pm each evening, and even the automatic locks close for the French lunch.

The Vendange—men on small tractors pulling yellow trailers full of future wine—a promise to be fulfilled. The wind bubbling in arouses the flags ... Morning has broken: Wake up.

Mother duck and chicks float by looking for that first meal as her ladyship fulfills a mother's role in providing for her children. The church bell chimes ... 7:00 am. Tom rejoins me on the deck with a bowl of tea, lovingly ladled from a pot. Morning has broken: Illumination, colours, water, and ideas. Trees saluting the wind.

A farmer's white *petit* Renault truck traverses the path on the left bank at 7:30. Late for the *vendange*! Or perhaps early for the warm baguettes at the *Capestang boulangerie*, delivered with love and respect exactly at *huit heures*. Sudden movements on the Connoisseur boat, moored beside us. In an instance, a fleeting glance, brief smile, slight wave, a diesel motor, flying ropes, and they are gone. An early bird to catch which worm? The village is still quiet.

Nothing opens until 8:00 am. Sun miraculously breaks through the *nuage* and the wind overcomes the fortress wall of plane trees. The tricolour flags are fully awake. The canal surface ripples and glistens in a daily ritual of song and dance. The sweet sounds of the pump crunching and pushing our daily essence into the water adds the only discordance. Is this the way to treat a World Heritage Site?

Retirement has some virtues and the Moorea eventually comes to life in its own time. Powering up to our massive, overpowering five klicks, we set off for Beziers. Not to worry. Traffic light ... Poilhes on the left and right ... Hot sun. Little stirs. Cannons on the wharf go unchallenged.

Musings from a Boat on the Canal du Midi, 2006

What's that ahead? The canal seems to enter a black hole. Steady, Captain Rod, steady.

Hold that red. Sound the horn. Again and again. No response. All is quiet. Disaster avoided ... In we go. There's light at the end of the tunnel reflected in the pitted, pocked limestone rock. No moss or lichens darken this arid ceiling. No need for prayer—red wine maybe, after all there is plenty more where that came from ... the hand does need to be steady.

Miraculously no incursion blocks the passage, and we are safe. Surely a given, as Moorea's safe passage had been precedent, uncounted times since 1641.

Saturday, September 16th, 4:00 pm:

Oops, we didn't understand the fluvial guide. Here we are, stranded in Beziers— must await another dawning. But still, the night will not be totally wasted, although we might be ... the regional crafty touristy shop sells Rose. Cheers ! Hic.

Sunday 17th:

The dawn approaches stealthily, unpretentiously, careful not to surprise us with the potential brilliance of the day; there are no clouds to veil its pending magnificence. Eight boats line up to do battle with the rushing, gushing, water of the locks. Work, strain, pool, shout, rush, strain, sweat, sway, gusty, tighten, throw, release, sigh. Only five more to go. Thirty minutes, six locks, avoid the car partly submerged at the bottom.

Team play: We're there.

Beziers: Large. Bright. Clean. Quiet. Traffic. . Breadless. Shopless. Ulster Sunday. Broken water connections. Powerless. Bike rides. Alouette tour boat. Cathedral Saint Nazaire on high.

Musings from a Boat on the Canal du Midi, 2006

Too much work for so little reward. Push on.

Agde. Canal bank, slippery slope, embankment, insects Sounds, Montpellier trackers, love Canada, Quebec, long chat in French, Ian the Englishman from Sniowdonia stops by for a chat, Railway brasserie for supper, traffic, traffic, noise, damn two strokes, twits, trains, slow trains, fast trains, Sunday rush hours, special mussels and *frites*, eight-euros, gay waiter, casual English speaker, Rod/ Sue chastised for not finishing their *Plat du Jour*, an unidentified bird mincing, prancing, a wild flourish and dessert and coffee for some, laughter, mirth, giggles and laughter, and a long walk back in the dark.

Monday, September 18th:

Morning gently brushes Agde. By 7:00 the silence ends in a swirl of diesel engines as the basin comes alive. Human voices penetrate the still air. Whistle. Whistle. Agitated call. A short stocky Frenchman calls to a hiding, petrified hound. Someone collars the dog, which collapses on the ground. The short stocky French animal lover hauls the dog by the neck and alternatively slaps it and shouts. Carol has to be physically restrained. Which is just as well as the dog owner turns out to be the lockkeeper, late for work. Wonder why he is late? Pastis? Assignation? Late for the only round lock in the system.

The Englishman from Wales stops by for a chat and to ask questions on the operation of the circular *ecluse*. He settles in for a natter. The only problem is that I am stark naked beside the window off the cabin, unable to move without being seen. I had to call Tom who was about to wax poetically on some issue in order to obtain a towel without ;revealing it all. After a night of River Rats, imagined or not, it made my reservations about mooring with the window facing alongside the land very real.

Musings from a Boat on the Canal du Midi, 2006

Tuesday 19th:

Marseillan in the morning—Swallows leave their nests in the tiled roofs. Shadows on the cream walls of the cave cooperatives. The blue door echoing the blue wrought iron balconies off the *Rococo Château de Port* with its Guardian Liberty and her crown lights looking out for all who sail here.

We appreciated the Guardian Liberty on the rough ride to Bouzigues the next day. Tom, as the only non-swimmer, is somewhat anxious even though the water was only four-feet deep. Captain Rod navigated with skill obviously inherited from his father, a former Shell supertanker captain, through the famous oyster beds, and we arrive at Boutiques around 2:00 pm.

Quiet afternoon reading, sipping rose, followed by an oyster meal, which was a shock to some. *There's no better way to spend the day,* says a distinguished Frenchman passing with his elegant wife.

Nothing much to do here, says a crusty Geordie.

Wednesday 29th:

Forecast sunny and calm, much appreciated. Up Before Dawn to watch the Sun on the shoreline come to life. Fisher folk in dowh-like boats off to tend the oyster beds. Gulls squawk and row. No early tractors tending the *vendange* here.

The day arrives in an instance, No transitions here. Water glistens gently in the breeze. Off to the lift bridge at Frontignan. Where is the canal entrance? They have it well disguised.

At last it announces itself, and we glide through the mixed zone of cozy Fisher cottages with nets drying in the razor sharp sun interspersed between refineries with hundreds of one leg flamingos feeding in the shallow

Musings from a Boat on the Canal du Midi, 2006

etangs. At last the bridge. When will it open? Tied up waiting and waiting in front of the vertical Iron Bridge—ten heaving beasts, bilges bursting. Anxious German Helmsman wiping their furrowed brows.

They must be first ... must be first, or at least be in the proper order.

At last the mystery is solved; the bridge ascends not at 1:00 pm, as listed in the fluvial guide, or at 1:30, as posted on the bridge, but at 1:48—as posted nowhere. Is this a sign of the decay in the Fifth Republic? We bring up the rear, as is befitting the laid back tenacious Canucks, whose presence seems to bring a smile to many.

In truth, we would rather have the Germans and Swiss ahead of us. Who needs a Graf Spey[1] up the arse.

Many women fish along the canal but never in the company of men. Men and women who stay together don't fish together. Why is this ? Would they talk at each other too much and distract the fish? Would one be telling the other what to do? Too many crossed wires? Perhaps each needs peace and solitude from time to time.

Except for the putt ... putt ... putt of the diesel river boats.

---

[1] The Graf Spey was a very large German Battleship in WW2 that the Allies spent a very large effort to trap in the estuary of the Rio Platte.

Chapter XX

Myth and Reality

When does reality become mythology and can mythology become reality? These are questions I asked myself after my first trip to the Georgian Republic, and therefore behind the Iron Curtain.

On my trips to The Georgian Republic, I chose to board with Georgian families. What better way to connect to Georgia and discover what makes her click. I discovered a land and people soaked in history, from the burial site of the earliest hominids in Europe, to the possible birthplace of wine-making some 7000 years ago.

I didn't even know that Georgians made wine, but now, having consumed a litre or two or three, I am fully convinced. My purpose in visiting Georgia was to help a small business develop a business plan in order to expand the operation.

The problem was that the owners of this language school had a daughter studying at the London School of Economics, and every penny they made went to her education, so nothing came of my business suggestions. I did however meet some interesting people, some of whom are friends to this day.

The flights to Tbilisi are amongst the last to leave Heathrow, and I don't believe that there are any discount airlines flying to Georgia. As a result there are few tourists, and it isn't on many peoples must-visit list. This has not been helped by the current political issues (2025) and the fact that Georgia was once part of the Soviet Union, which Putin seems to want to revive.

The Russians invaded part of Georgia in 2008 and are still there ... guaranteeing Peace????????? An early alert for Ukraine, perhaps.

Myth and Reality

Me and My Guitar

My first host had been a foreign service employee of the Soviet Union and now worked in insurance. As a student he had been a member of a rock band called Mao and Friends. They had been investigated by the KGB for anti-Soviet Activities. When I was there the band still existed and played once a year, but on many Sundays,

Myth and Reality

they rehearsed in a soundproofed room at the Technical University, a room to which they have the only key. Hanging on the wall was an early Gibson guitar worth about $40,000.

I went along one Sunday for the experience, and an experience it was. When they heard that I once taught at a school that Bruce Cockburn attended, they became really excited. A few friends from their high school days showed up (original groupies) as did bread, cheese, meat, beer and *grappa*, and the party began.

I skyped Eileen later that evening, and the first thing that she said was, *you're smashed, I can smell the booze*.

Later, I went to a Sunday open air market in Tbilisi with my host. It was a combined flea market, a general goods market and an arts and crafts market. Georgia is for many citizens a cash-poor economy. There are rich, some hangovers from Soviet days who managed to get their hands on parts of the economy.

A good friend of mine, Maka, has really tried to become an independent business person, but the obstacles are enormous, and the banks charge very high rates for borrowing. Advertising is also expensive, so people get dressed up in their Sunday best, pin a picture of the fridge, car, anything they want to sell, and circulate until they meet a likely buyer.

I was interested in sculpture, but found the pieces on display to be expensive. Upon talking to an artist, he suggested that my friend and I visit his studio, where he could give us a better deal. A few nights later we made our way up into the hills that surround Tbilisi. Even the taxi driver got lost. Finally sequestered in a converted garage, wandering around pieces of rock and breathing the dust-filled air, we came to an impasse. He wanted me to buy a large piece that would cost a fortune in air freight,

Myth and Reality

The Good Ship Argo

Myth and Reality

and I didn't need a statue of the Virgin Mary. Also he did not appear as friendly as in our earlier meeting.

Then a door opened. In a corner covered in dust I saw a small piece that appeared to be a ship. He told us that while walking on a Black Sea beach he had found a nice rock that he was sure he could use. It stayed unused for about five years until he was inspired to bring forth '*The Good Ship: Argo*', from Greek mythology, Jason and the Argonauts, and The Golden Fleece.

Now for reality. That part of Georgia is called Svaneti in the northwestern part of the country, and is a part of the Greater Caucasus Mountain Range. It is a very striking region, sometimes known as the Land of 1000 Towers, and I would have loved for it to be a part of my journey, but alas it was not to be. The inhabitants have for centuries panned for gold using sheep stomachs. Is that the origin of the Golden Fleece? Myth or reality? I wonder every time I look at the lovely limestone carving sitting on my coffee table.

By the way, Eileen loved it as it is a lovely carved piece of polished limestone with some fossils emphasizing the ship's features.

You could tell that I loved these journeys. As soon as I made an offer and placed some cash on a table, the whole atmosphere changed. His son emerged from the house with a small table, to be followed by his wife with plates of cooked meats, bread, and cheese. The son reappeared with a flagon of homemade red wine ... all good, and the sculptor started telling us stories of the Soviet days. He was originally from a farm in Svaneti, where you could have any type of farm equipment as long as it was made in the Soviet Union.

Now with the Soviets long gone, there are no spare parts and the equipment is useless, with the resulting decline in farm production. New equipment is too expensive, and bank loans are exorbitant. ... Out came another flagon of wine. It was possibly the best homemade wine I had ever tasted, and until a few weeks previous, I had no idea that wine was made in Georgia, nor that it may originally have been the home of wine-making.

One aspect of Georgian life that does not appeal to me is the ultraconservative Georgian Orthodox Church. For one thing, unless you are an invalid, you have to stand. The Church is incredibly homophobic, to the extent that priests have been seen egging on youth gangs to attack Pride parades. One wonders if the power of the current church stems from the fact that under the Soviets, church attendance was seriously discouraged and with the Fall of the Soviet Union, people fell back to dependence on older male-centric institutions, remnants of a former time.

It was a shock to me, when I saw middle-aged women on hands and knees scrubbing the church floors, but they cannot enter the Inner Sanctum. It reminded me of poor Tibetans dragging themselves in the dirt around Stupas outside the Buddhist temples, and I wondered why? Is California the new home of spiritual Buddhists while the suffering Buddhists are dragging themselves in the dirt?

I worked in Georgia a second time to assist a friend in the creation of the Georgian Canadian Education Centre, offering courses in languages and computers. The family I was with this time were wealthier and had two vehicles, which resulted in me seeing more of the countryside in this ancient land, which acted as a corridor between East and West throughout history.

When I left this time, I was bombarded with gifts from homemade wine, a honey comb to a full case of bought wine. I was away overweight at check in but explained

Myth and Reality

that it was the result of Georgian hospitality. She laughed, placed a heavy case sticker on my suitcase and did not charge me ... another successful stop en-route.

Like Georgia, I visited Ukraine twice. The first time I was based at the University of Pereyaslav, and was asked to draw up an ecotourism plan for the community. There were so many question marks about this project that I feel, given that this is a war-torn nation, I should restrict my comments. Suffice to say I was supposed to be there for five weeks, and with the help of Eileen and some new Ukrainian friends, I left after three ... work completed. The signature on the proposal documents was that of a local bar/restaurant owner, whom I was assured was more of a mafia figure without the slightest interest in ecotourism. In addition, my local contact person, whom I never met in Ukraine, was paid for every day I remained there and was unable or unwilling to help me when I requested assistance.

Despite the apparent makeshift organization there were some successes, such as great people, including my interpreters, a great Professor of Linguistics, who went out of her way to assist me. Without her help, I could not have completed the assignment. I trust that she is still in Czechna.

I do have a fairy tale type story to tell from this visit, one that is quite unexpected and ongoing. Masha, the Linguistics Prof, asked me if I would talk to a group of students studying English. This I did, and at the end a group of students gathered at the front with questions. At one point a student asked if I had ever tried Ukrainian beer? I should add that it was very hot. Off we went to a local bar for some light refreshment and a few more hours of English chat.

Myth and Reality

At about 7:30 pm the group began to dissipate, and I realized that I was off campus, had no idea how to find my university residence, and of course did not speak Ukrainian. At this point a young lady and a guy said that they would escort me back. Off we went and had barely gone 200 m when the young man remembered that he had to be somewhere. Alina said that she would see me safe and even helped me shop for some food supplies. Outside my building we chatted for a bit and I gave her my card.

Alina and her two young children, Isabella and Sebastien, have been living as my guest in Orillia since September 2022, where they have become treasured members of my family. About three months after I arrived back in Toronto, I received a letter and some poetry she had written, plus an email address. We remained in contact over the years, and two weeks before Putin INVADED Ukraine, I invited her and her family to be my guests in Orillia. She thanked me, but said that they thought that the war would last only a few weeks. Six months later after the nightmare of Canadian immigration, never mind the war and the need to exit quickly, my daughter, Kelly, and I picked them up at Pearson Airport.

I can honestly say that Alina has not looked back. The kids, who did not speak English, are now so fluent one would not know that they were foreign born. They are now an integral part of my family. One would also have to say that the people she has been in contact with have been great, and Monsignor Lee School has been marvellous.

My second trip was quite different in that I was in charge of a Canadian election observation team in the current war torn Oblast of Zaphoritzia. In my humble opinion this was not a truly serious operation and its major goal was to show the Canadian flag to the Ukrainian electorate at home. Am I being too harsh? Why then was

Myth and Reality

my team pulled out in the middle of the election count, which lasted all night, in order for us to attend a celebration party at the embassy, where we even had to buy our own beer.

The party was somewhat subdued as the Ukrainian Canadians were depressed as the candidate they liked, lost. Personally I was not sure what difference it would have made as Putin supported both of them. I was very proud of my team, most of whom were Ukrainian speakers. I cooperated with a European Union group, whose leader had been there for 4 months. I had been instructed not to, but what the h***, why not?

He had every polling station covered but one, so I lent him two of my team so that we had foreign observers in every poll. My team was involved in all my decisions, and they appreciated it. Before we left Kiev I had to calm a revolt as the incompetent organizers, who I believed were playing games, sent us on a 20-hour bus ride, on a bus without a working toilet, as the owner/driver could not afford antifreeze. Did I mention that this was February? When our sole female member had to go to the bathroom, the men formed a circle on the road looking outward; the bus driver shut the lights off, and she crouched within the circle ... tinkle, tinkle.

On another occasion one of the men headed towards a shack in the distance. I insisted he take a flashlight and that was fortunate as the shack turned out to be a fishing hut on the Dnieper River. He might have drowned.

Enough said. I made a full report to the organizers, and shut the door behind me as I never heard from them again. I feel good though ... to thyself be true, and I did try and save the Canadian taxpayer some money, which the organizers seemed to want to spend more in Ukraine than was necessary. Where relatives are involved, who knows?

Myth and Reality

My journey to Eastern Europe also included working in Serbia and Armenia, and these followed a similar track. Interesting clients: e.g., in Serbia my client was originally an engineer, who designed military tanks for Tito's army in the former Yugoslavis and now operates three separate language schools. —Clients, who want certain things, but when faced with reality fall back into their old ways— Great hospitality, good food, trips to the countryside, and the Opera.

Interesting times, great people, and some unattainable agendas, but what can one do ... leave them smiling and continue the scenic journey through the next door.

Patrick at the castle

XXI

Family Jaunts

No lifetime journey would be complete without reference to an all-time family favourite, the annual vacation and sometimes the day trips to places like Niagara Falls, African Lion Safari, baseball games and the Canadian National Exhibition. Further Canadian trips regularly took us to Almonte, Ontario, to visit Eileen's grandmother, Nana Rose, and to Montreal to see family and friends. We have visited both coasts, including Newfoundland, but not the bit in the middle, with the exception of Calgary and Edmonton. We are all dual citizens, both Irish and Canadian, which means we are European as well. Somehow that feels very refreshing in these times.

We have had more than a few trips to Ireland, both North and South, and met some great people, both my parents, sister, Betty and husband, David and their sons, Paul and Ian and his family. None greater than Charters and Ethel and their sons, John, Michael and George, who were part of Eileen's grandmother's family that had continuously worked the farm since 1604.

The farm was known as The Rock and Charters had a dynamite license during the troubles to break up the glacially deposited rocks, so abundant amongst the clay soils. Charters was one of those salt-of-the-Earth farmers who once said to us that, *A man who can make two blades of grass grow, where previously only one had grown, has made a far greater contribution to this earth than any politician.*

We have also visited Cuba five times and keep going back. Sure there are issues from time to time, but the people seem to generally appreciate Canadian visitors; the

Family Jaunts

weather usually great, and the all-inclusive deals take the pressure off finding places to eat.

Although it may hurt me as an Irishman, having seen a sign in London that read,

NO DOGs OR IRISH WELCOME

I do have some great English friends, especially the Dorset crowd of Sally and family and her ex, who lives not far away on a 17th Century Manor and farm. Great people and a wonderful compliment on our journey.

Last but not least, I must include the adventures we had with our good friends, Rod and Sue Henderson. We did month-long house exchanges in Glasgow and just north of Nice, plus a long stay in Portugal, and several trips to Cuba. Great travelling companions, and a pleasure to share life's journey with.

Chapter XXII

Les Belles Isles

Islands have always been important to me. I was born on one: Ireland. My first sight of Canada was Newfoundland. Our first family adventure was to Trinidad, and while there we spent some time in Tobago. While in the Southern/Eastern Caribbean, we visited Barbados, Margarita, and Grenada. For Eileen and my 25th wedding anniversary, Kelly, Ken, and Patrick sent us to The Bahamas. In 2023, I visited Iceland with Kelly, and in 2024, revisited with our family friend, Sally. In 1994, I had a contract to assist in The Philippines, where I went fishing on the South China Sea under a full moon, which never seemed so huge, and where I had to hide under the kitchen table when my hosts thought that there were Maoist rebels in the village. The journey was a little sticky at times. Any reference to islands would not be complete without a reference to the home of Beausoleil First Nation, Christian Island, in Georgian Bay.

Along with family and friends we have spent over 30 years in joint communion with humanity and nature, sometimes pensively, sometimes with great festivity, and always ending the summer season with the Lane Potluck ... great friends ... great times. We are also grateful for our friends in the local Indigenous Community. Spending time on the beach at Big Sand Bay, walking through the Cathedral of the Trees, and conversing with the Grandfather Rocks with family close at hand ... Is there a better place to be? —Especially with our granddaughter, Meghan and Adam's Beach wedding scheduled for July of 2025, and the first great-grandchild, Sage, and our grandson, Liam and partner Dominique, to share it all with.

Les Belles Isles

One cannot talk about the cottage without referring to the superb changes made to it over the years through the craft skills of Ken, our son-in-law, a perfectionist at heart. A perfect closure of this stage of a life that has been wonderful.

As I said at Eileen's Celebration of Life, a road well travelled ... ALONG THE SCENIC ROUTE.

Appendix

As humans, who walk on land, we are quite accustomed to ignoring the fact that approximately 74% of the planet consists of water, and I feel that it would be remiss of not to include the oceans, seas, lakes, and rivers that have touched me in some way on the scenic journey:

Rivers: Lagan, Upper and Lower Bann, the Foyle, Boyne, Liffey, Shannon Clyde, Forth, Tweed, Dee, Thames, Severn, Avon, Seine, Loire, Garonne, Rhône, Elbe, Danube, Canal du Midi, Canal du Narbonne, Kura/Mrkvari, Dnieper, Hwang Ho, Yangtze, Nile, Mara, Orinoco, Marowijne, St Lawrence, Ottawa, Don, Humber

Large bodies of water: North Atlantic Ocean, North Pacific Ocean, North Sea, Irish Sea, English Channel, Bay of Biscay, Mediterranean Sea, Baltic Sea, Black Sea, Sea of Azov, South China Sea, Caribbean Sea, Gulf of Mexico, The Great Lakes.

Now we can add some volcanic activity such as active volcanoes, Mount Arenal, Mount Pinatubo, and Poas. Then there are the current dyke type eruptions of the Reykjanes Peninsula in Iceland.

Lastly we can add some of the great mountain regions: The Rockies, the various Alps, The Caucasus, The Pyrenees, The Appalachians, the Scottish Highlands, and upland areas such as: the Black Forest, Massif Central, the Meseta, the Canadian Shield, the Tibetan Plateau, and the East African Plateau and the Great Rift Valley.

There were obviously, others smaller but locally no less significant, and they have all exposed the geographer that lies buried within me.

Afterword

In 2011 as a foreign language English student in Ukraine I was told by my teacher to attend the lecture by native English speaker. It was Tom, and I was captured by his ability to tell the greatest stories! He does not simply share them; he teleports not only himself, but everybody around to different places and times, with a smile, and sometimes, with a glass of Red or White.

We stayed in touch through many years via emails and Facebook Messenger, but in 2022 we met in person again after the Russian invasion of Ukraine.

Our family merged in the past three years, and I am delighted to listen to fascinating adventures all over the world, often, and in person.

If you love stories, you will definitely travel vicariously as you read this book!

Alina Hromko
Professional Photographer

www.ingramcontent.com/pod-product-compliance
Lightning Source LLC
Chambersburg PA
CBHW050815160426
43192CB00010B/1776